## World Comics and Graphic Nonfiction Series

# The Claremont Run

## *Subverting Gender in the X-Men*

J. Andrew Deman

Foreword by Jay Edidin

University of Texas Press

*Austin*

Requests for permission to reproduce material from this work should be sent to:
    Permissions
    University of Texas Press
    P.O. Box 7819
    Austin, TX 78713-7819
    utpress.utexas.edu

∞ The paper used in this book meets the minimum requirements of ANSI/
NISO Z39.48-1992 (R1997) (Permanence of Paper).

Library of Congress Cataloging-in-Publication Data

Names: Deman, J. Andrew, author.
Title: The Claremont run : subverting gender in the X-Men / J. Andrew Deman.
Other titles: World comics and graphic nonfiction series.
Description: First edition. | Austin : University of Texas Press, 2023. | Series:
    World comics and graphic nonfiction series | Includes bibliographical
    references and index.
Identifiers: LCCN 2022062220 (print) LCCN 2022062221 (ebook)
    ISBN 978-1-4773-2545-2 (hardcover)
    ISBN 978-1-4773-2546-9 (pdf)
    ISBN 978-1-4773-2547-6 (epub)
Subjects: LCSH: Claremont, Chris, 1950—Criticism and interpretation. |
    Claremont, Chris, 1950—Characters. | Claremont, Chris, 1950—Influence. |
    X-men (Comic strip)—Characters. | Women superheroes in comics. |
    Sex role in comics. | Superheroes in comics. | Gender identity in comics. |
    LCGFT: Comics criticism.
Classification: LCC PN6727.C55 Z58 2023 (print) | LCC PN6727.C55
    (ebook) | DDC 741.5/973—dc23/eng/20230111
LC record available at https://lccn.loc.gov/2022062220
LC ebook record available at https://lccn.loc.gov/2022062221

doi:10.7560/325452

*To Andrea, for her love and support, and to Aria and Amara, who deserve every granular gain in our society that this comic book author might have contributed toward "the utopian dream of the hope for a monstrous world without gender."*

*To X-Twitter, for inspiring in me a love of public-facing scholarship and for helping me understand the limits of the ivory tower.*

*To Charley, Scott, Jean, Ororo, Logan, Peter, Kurt, Sean, Kitty, Rogue, Betsy, Alex, Ali—and all the rest—and to Chris Claremont for the breath of life he provided them.*

# Contents

# A Danger Room of One's Own

Jay Edidin

My *X-Men* summer fell between my sophomore and junior years of college. Excited for some measure of independence and desperate to avoid sinking into the slow, sticky misery of Florida summers, my boyfriend and I had gotten jobs on campus. First, though, we'd made a brief pilgrimage back home, and when we went back north, we brought a stack of long boxes—his childhood comics collection, and his dad's before that.

I'd read *X-Men* comics before, sporadically, with no particular attention to continuity or creators. That summer, I dug in for the long haul. I read; and *X-Men* summer turned into *X-Men* fall as I opened a pull box at the local comics shop. I read; and that winter, I scoured the internet and dollar bins for back issues.

If you'd asked me then what had grabbed me so firmly, I'm not sure I could have told you. It wasn't until the following spring, reading Virginia Woolf's "A Room of One's Own," that I realized exactly what I had latched on to.

"A Room of One's Own" is a treatise on Woolf's experience as a woman within—or, more accurately, at the margins of—the aggressively male-dominated literary establishment. Later, it also delves into literature by women—specifically, a novel that strikes Woolf as fairly mediocre until she stumbles across a passage that reads, "Chloe liked Olivia. They shared a laboratory together."

Here is the truth Woolf homes in on: It is one thing to write female characters who have genuine interiority. It is something else altogether—and something far rarer—to write female characters who genuinely like each other.

Which brings me to Chris Claremont.

Among many aspects of his work, Claremont is famous—justly famous—for dimensional and dynamic female characters, to the extent that "Claremont women" has become semantic shorthand within the spheres of superhero comics. The female *X-Men* he redefined (Storm,

Jean Grey) or created from whole cloth (Shadowcat, Rogue, Psylocke, and many more) are iconic in their own right. Even Claremont's female villains are unusually nuanced, as compelling and complex as his heroines.

But what matters more are their relationships.

Critics and fans—including me—have talked a lot about the lesbian subtext in Claremont's *X-Men*; and, look, there's a *lot* of it. But what we often neglect to mention is that those queer-reading couples are part of a broader spectrum of deep and complex relationships between women in his work. Claremont's women love each other and like each other. They are friends; they are barely subtextual lovers; they are literal or surrogate sisters or mothers or daughters. They are rivals, sometimes, but with enmity as faceted and compelling as their friendships.

If you have spent your comics-reading life identifying as male, you may not understand why this is revolutionary. Listen: When you are a female-identifying person—as I was when I started reading *X-Men*—a lifetime of fiction has told you that the only way to be a hero is to be alone. You have learned that the girls who succeed are *not like the other girls*; that, indeed, if you want to succeed, you will need to reject everything that defines your gender, including any peers unlucky enough to share it. You have learned that other women are deadweight at best, but more often rivals, and—look, you get the idea.

And then, maybe, if you're lucky, you read Claremont's *X-Men*.

"Chloe liked Olivia"—in the world of spandex and super heroics, it could just as easily be "Jean liked Ororo," or "Polaris liked Rogue." The spaces they share are unshadowed by their male teammates, even when those teammates more often end up in the popular spotlight. *They openly admire each other*, and if you don't understand how much that means, how rare that is, I would wager that you don't quite understand *X-Men*.

All of this is a long-winded way of saying that, for me, Claremont's *X-Men* has always been about gender, represented in ways I had never seen in another superhero comic, even decades after it was first published. It's been nearly twenty years since my *X-Men* summer turned into my *X-Men* fall, then grew into a far larger lens for what I was hungry for in stories and the world around me. And now, finally, you no longer have to flip back a century to Virginia Woolf or look to metaphors for what you find in mutants. You have, in your hands, a text that speaks to exactly that.

It's about time.

Jay Edidin
Forest Hills, NY (Yes, the place where Spider-Man lives)

# THE CLAREMONT RUN

# X-Women to Watch Out For

There was a moment I think when I made a conscious decision by looking around seeing how few people were portraying heroic rational sensible women in books and comics. I thought, "I'll fill that vacuum–since no one else is doing it, I'll give it a try." Because in a sense I wondered in the ultimate kind of fiction, science fiction, could I put myself in the head of this being who was totally unlike me?

–CHRIS CLAREMONT, QUOTED IN PETER SANDERSON, *THE X-MEN COMPANION II*

The world of superhero comics has largely been a highly gendered universe with a clear sense of normative and nonnormative be- haviors for both men and women while very much positing that relationship between genders as binary and exclusive: two genders, two paradigms of expected behavior, rarely anything between or outside of those opposing poles. And within that binary is a clear and resolute hier- archy of subordination defining the relationship between male and female characters, each overdetermined by gender. This extreme and essential- ist interpretation of gender became so entrenched that any challenges to its hegemony were most likely to come from the margins of the industry, rather than from the most popular titles. But there was one particularly notable exception to this pattern at Marvel comics.

From 1975 to 1991, Chris Claremont wrote *Uncanny X-Men*, forming the longest stint of any writer on a single title in Marvel's history. During his tenure, *X-Men* went from a B-list title on the verge of cancellation to the best-selling comic book in the world, and Claremont still holds the Guinness World Record for the best-selling single-issue comic of all time (Glenday 300). In addition, *X-Men* is widely considered "one of the most socially relevant and diverse superhero comic book titles" (Schedeen n.p.). It is from this rare position of prominence that Claremont's *X-Men* was able to explore gender roles in ways that comics critics and scholars have taken notice of. As famous comics scribe and feminist media critic Gail Simone points out, "the biggest sea change in female superheroes ever came from Marvel, with the X-Men. I think that changed the rules for the better for everyone" (@GailSimone n.p.). The foundational comics scholar Bradford W. Wright also notes how Claremont's simple incorporation of strong female characters "helped to expand the title's appeal across the gender barrier, and *The X-Men* became one of the very few superhero titles to win a significant female following" (qtd. in Darowski, *X-Men* 11).

Thus Claremont's run is considered very successful, and importantly progressive in its gender representation, but we have to add that his run was also unusually long, making it very difficult to approach as a subject. How can you even discuss, debate, describe, and study a comics story that was sixteen years in the making? As Jason Powell notes, "No one has duplicated that length of time on a mainstream superhero comic. Factor in all the X-related spin-off series, and the total sum begins to approach somewhere around 380 comics" (274); however, what seems like a challenge can actually be spun into an advantage. While the enormity of Claremont's run makes it difficult to broach, it does provide a truly unique sample of comics writing, one of incomparable size. Thus, as a subject of content analysis, there is a lot that we can do with it.

For this book, I drew substantial data from the first holistic academic studies of Claremont's work at a watershed moment in Claremont studies. His work was first discussed by early comics scholars in the 1990s (Reynolds, Sabin), but Claremont studies did not become a focus of comics scholarship until around 2013. The ramp-up to this rediscovery of Claremont's work has been impressive. The big three have been Cocca, Darowski (*X-Men*), and Fawaz, published in 2016, 2014, and 2016, respectively. Whereas Cocca situates Claremont as a central voice in the history of the superheroine particularly, Darowski explores the broader social metaphors implicit in Claremont's work, and Fawaz engages primarily with the concept of "queer mutanity" (queer-coding) through Claremont's writing. Each of these studies focuses on a particular discourse, yet each author is identifying a thread of social progressivism and subversion within Claremont's work. This is appropriate given the impressive accomplishments of his run, which features, among other things, the first African American superheroine (Cocca 125), the first black superhero team leader (Darowski, *X-Men* 78), the first canonically Jewish superhero (Cronin), extensive queer subtext (Fawaz 35), extensive BDSM (bondage, domination, submission, and masochism) imagery (Howe 77), the first superhero team with a strong female roster (Powell 73), the best-selling single-issue comic of all time (Glenday 300), and of course the longest continuous run by a single author in Marvel's history (Powell 6).

The holistic perspective that this project takes is not just for the sake of being comprehensive, but for the sake of understanding what it is about the Claremont run that truly makes its representation of gender impact-ful and even enduring. Claremont's work has achieved a higher level of symbolic capital in our culture in recent years than arguably that of any of his contemporaries. Jay Edidin and Miles Stokes have spent years on their podcast, *Jay and Miles X-Plain the X-Men*, analyzing Claremont's work on an issue-by-issue basis, and the podcast has achieved wild popularity. According to Box Office Mojo, the thirteen-movie *X-Men* film franchise from 20th Century Fox generated $6 billion in revenue. Marvel continues to reprint the run in a wide number of formats and collected editions.

My project here provides an important missing piece to the study of Claremont's work through the holistic, evidence-based perspective that it adds to our popular culture's thirst for discussion, adaptation, and ap-preciation of Claremont's most important writing and the impact it had on social perspectives on gender performance and gender identity. This evidence includes a combination of quantitative content-analysis data and qualitative interpretation within what John Cresswell defines as a mixed-methods sequential explanatory design. Within this structure, "the researcher first conducts quantitative research, analyzes the results and then builds on the results to explain them in more detail with qualita-tive research" (15). Simply put, data is constructed first and then used to prompt the qualitative analysis that follows, thus creating more rigorous lines of inquiry. This approach differs from traditional quantitative studies, which use data to "prove" rather than to "prompt." In any mixed-methods approach, data can do both—thus empowering the qualitative compo-nent without relegating all interpretive findings to raw numbers. And, indeed, although the study I undertake here launches from these data points, the focus thereafter becomes analytical reading, comparison, and the application of literary theory (particularly comics scholarship, as one might expect).

With the financial support of St. Jerome's University and the Social Sciences and Humanities Research Council (SSHRC) of Canada, my team and I conducted content analysis on Chris Claremont's sixteen-year run on *Uncanny X-Men* comics in order to create data sets for future schol-ars to study (myself included). The process entailed page-by-page anal-ysis of Claremont's run on *Uncanny X-Men* (*UXM*) issue nos. 97–278,[1] gathering quantitative information on structure, characterization, and representation. I also conducted research at Columbia University, where I cross-referenced my initial findings with Claremont's personal papers, which are archived in Columbia University's Rare Book and Manuscript Library. In addition, I interviewed Claremont over the phone in order to generate some initial perspectives on his process. As the project came together, I initiated a micro-publishing portfolio through social media to share my findings and interpretations with the broader community of *X-Men* readers, fans, critics, scholars, and creators through a Twitter account under the handle @ClaremontRun. That has provided this project with endlessly beneficial dialogue, support, insight, and community, for which I am deeply grateful.

The central focus of this project is, however, gender. Although the isolation of gender in Claremont's work can be described as "single-axis"—which Patrick R. Grzanka defines as "those perspectives, methods, and modes of analysis that privilege one dimension of inequality (e.g., race or gender or class)" (xv)—said isolation of gender as a variable can provide some insight into the binary world that Claremont operates within Marvel comics of the 1970s and 1980s. Patrick Hogan, in *Sexual Identities*, notes that exploring gender binaries need not be seen as a betrayal of constructionist viewpoints because characters in many stories are identified as male or female, and "are trained in—or coerced into—putatively masculine or feminine behaviors" (3). Thus, for Hogan, analyzing gender within highly gendered fantasy worlds can actually be quite productive by considering the terms upon which the fictional world is built while creating opportunities to undermine it through the identification of gender deviancy, an approach that is central to my reading methodology in the chapters ahead.

Gender can also serve as a grounding point for representational analysis, allowing us to branch out into intersectional analysis of a deeply intersectional run. Indeed, we might see Claremont's integration of other social categories in his depiction of gender as a major contributing factor to both the complexity of the characters he cultivates and to the broader deviation from established gender norms in comics that Claremont can be seen to undertake. As with many aspects of the Claremont run, the character of Storm (a black, bisexual orphan/goddess) leads the way.

Consider, for example, Deborah Whaley's reading of Eartha Kitt's impact on the 1960s *Batman* television series:

> A critical mass of viewers could and did view the roles of Catwoman's lackeys, Manks and Angora, as well as her comrades the Joker, the Riddler, and the Penguin, as powerful symbols of alternative white masculinity that did not rely upon hypermasculinity,

heterosexuality, or brute brawn to define their manhood. In this way, Kitt's appearance sets the stage for viewers to embrace a Catwoman whose blackness and allied relationship with unconventional white masculinities, without the insinuation of a sexual relationship, made her more socially significant in regard to the politics of race, gender, and sexualities. (78)

Whaley's description of Kitt's Catwoman could quite easily be applied to Storm, as can the complex intersections of blackness, sexuality, and gender and their subsequent impact, through relationality, on the portrayal of white masculinity in *X-Men* comics. In this manner, my readings are prompted by the analysis of gender in *X-Men* comics to speak to a much wider, interconnected system of representational politics.

Taking one of the most basic possible levels of representation as a quantitative launch point for the more complex and qualitative approaches of this project, I will first note that Claremont does extraordinarily well on the Bechdel test throughout his run on *UXM*. Though this is a controversial media-studies tool, the sheer size of the Claremont run as a data sample makes it uniquely well suited for Bechdel testing, and the results are compelling in their own right, creating a foundation from which to approach the nuanced components of Claremont's representation of gender in *X-Men* comics.

For the benefit of anyone who might be unfamiliar with this metric, the Bechdel test has been used extensively for determining whether or not a media work meets even a very low bar for representation of female characters. Alison Bechdel, a comics writer and artist, first coined the term in 1985 as part of her underground comic strip *Dykes to Watch Out For*. Bechdel herself would go on to play a significant role in the comics-as-literature movement with the publication of her book *Fun Home* in 2006.

The Bechdel test is not, however, the most precise measure of gender representation. Robbie Collin famously noted that the test has a tendency to simplify the complexity of representational concerns because "it prizes box-ticking and stat-hoarding over analysis and appreciation" (n.p.). For my part, I agree with Collin's assessment in principle; what I think he fails to consider (just as other opponents of the test might) is the value of a mixed-methods research methodology and the extent to which those ticked boxes can create or facilitate stronger discussions when paired with qualitative analysis. This is the approach used in my project.

Passing the Bechdel test does not indicate "good" gender representation, as many opponents of the test have suggested it is meant to. Rather, the test reveals a broad and pervasive pattern when applied to a large enough sample. It represents a minimum low bar that media can fail to surpass. Not every movie or comic book should be expected to pass the Bechdel test, but many of them should. When that is not happening, this tool can be a useful indicator of a general problem so long as the sample is large enough, and Claremont's run on *UXM* is as large as comics writers' samples get.

What makes the test so appropriate for this project is:

1. the fact that the Bechdel test is a binary metric—either pass or fail—and thus easily integrated and cross-referenced with other data sets from this project with little subjectivity
2. the alarming extent to which Marvel and DC comics of the Claremont era fail to pass the Bechdel test and thus the systemic patterns of misogyny that can be inferred

In order to pass the Bechdel test, (1) a work must have more than one female character; (2) the female characters must have a conversation with each other; and (3) the conversation has to be about something other than men. This is the original form of the Bechdel test. Later versions added the stipulation that the female characters who speak to each other must be named characters. For our purposes (again, in pursuing an already low bar), I opted to stick with the original iteration of the test, which is much easier on comics writers. In our study, the female characters did not have to be named in order to pass the Bechdel test, though I should note that Claremont's female characters usually are named, given his tendency to name all characters, even background ones, and all the works compared to Claremont's would come in with significantly lower numbers had we used the version of the test that requires names. All of this is to say that our application of the test disadvantages Claremont in this respect—yet still the numbers are compelling.

Of the *UXM* issues published during the Claremont run, 82 percent pass the Bechdel test (fig. 0.1). For contrast, the only major sales competition that Claremont had once *UXM* took off was from Frank Miller's work on *Daredevil* during two legendary arcs of that series centered around female characters: Elektra and Karen Page. Despite having these prominent female characters, not one of Miller's issues from either run passes the Bechdel test. Similarly disappointing is the work of other Claremont contemporaries. Only thirteen issues of Steve Englehart's famous forty-five-issue run on *Avengers* (1972–1976) passed (28 percent), and only eleven issues in Doug Moench's eighty-eight-issue run on *Master of Kung Fu* (1974–1983) passed (12.5 percent). For Moench's *Moon Knight* run (1980–1982), only one out of fifteen issues passed (7 percent).

If we focus just on *X-Men* comics, Claremont again stands out. In the first 500 issues of *UXM* (1963–2008), a pitiful 33 percent of the issues outside of Claremont's run passed the Bechdel test, with only four of sixty-six issues in the entire pre–Claremont run passing the test. During most of those pre-Claremont issues, the *UXM* team had only one female character (Jean Grey/Marvel Girl), and, as noted by Joseph Darowski, she was "one of the weakest members of a team dominated by patriarchal and fraternal attitudes" (*X-Men and the Mutant Metaphor* 45). For Darowski, this reflects a broader, "probably unintended pattern of subordination" in the series that relegates Jean to the margins through domestic symbols, subservient actions, diminutive identification in her code name (Marvel Girl rather than Marvel Woman),[2] sexualization, and internal motivations defined almost exclusively as romantic interest in male characters. This pattern is, of course, completely consistent with existing gender roles in comics of the time, and Claremont's turn away from them will be discussed in depth in the pages that follow, but it might be safe to say that women were never more central in *X-Men* comics than they were under Claremont.

These Bechdel scores have a limited currency, however. As mentioned earlier, if we look at the mechanics of the Bechdel test, it seems like a very low bar to surpass, and that is because it is. In isolation, the Bechdel test does not reveal which media artifacts have succeeded, just which ones have failed to meet a minimum standard; what is remarkable is the extent to which so many iconic and important cultural works do indeed fail to pass this test.

Most Marvel comics of the 1970s and 1980s, as you might suspect, fail the test, as our numbers show (fig. 0.1). In order to calculate a rough average, we Bechdel-tested every comic on Marvel Unlimited (Marvel's digital archive service) with a publication date corresponding to two months from each year between 1975 and 1990, and compared that to Claremont's Bechdel numbers for each of those years.

Despite the representative sample, the results are telling. Marvel output never clears 50 percent during this entire era, and we have to recall that Claremont (who passes with regularity) is actually included in that line-wide sample, thereby inflating the line-wide numbers. From this sample, we calculated the average discrepancy to be 42 percent. On average,

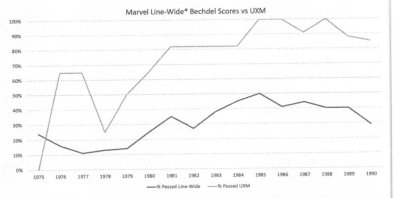

Marvel Line-Wide* Bechdel Scores vs UXM

——% Passed Line-Wide    ——% Passed UXM

*Marvel Line-Wide sample calculated algorithmically based on testing of all Marvel comics published
on Marvel Unlimited from two months (selected at random) from each year, including UXM.

**Fig. 0.1.** *Bechdel scores of the Claremont run of* Uncanny X-Men *issues versus scores of the entire Marvel line.*

each year, Claremont's issues were passing the Bechdel test 42 percent more often than the entire Marvel line (Claremont included).

These quantitative patterns are wholly consistent with some of the ways that Claremont's work has been isolated and discussed over the years in terms of his representation of women. Carol Cooper, for example, notes that "shifting attitudes toward sex and women became a big part of the book's increasing appeal once Claremont began scripting the X-Men" (195), and Ramzi Fawaz suggests that "*The X-Men* shifted the traditional locus of affective and political identification in mainstream superhero comics from white male heroes to powerful and racially diverse female superheroes" (147).

Although remarkable for the context Claremont was in, his work can be aligned with a broader countercultural movement that was emerging at the same time. Gender studies scholar R. W. Connell notes, for example, that with "the decline of political radicalism in the mid-1970s, the focus of counter-cultural life shifted towards introspection and personal relationships. By the early 1980s there was a well-developed therapeutic milieu devoted to personal growth and healing" (120). Appropriately, personal growth and healing are part of a wide number of character arcs throughout Claremont's tenure, often with specific thematic concerns on the impact of gender roles and expectations, a key subject that I will take up with individual character readings in the chapters that follow.

Historical accounts of the Marvel bullpen also confirm Claremont's atypical perspectives on gender. In the 1970s, Marvel was a bit of a boys' club, as thoroughly documented by Sean Howe in *Marvel Comics: The Untold Story*. Claremont, however, was a student of second-wave feminism at a time when this movement was radically altering the comics landscape, as noted by Hilary Chute, Charles Hatfield, and Susan Kirtley. Kirtley describes how second-wave feminism at the time was "paving the way for openly political discourse in the creative arts, while underground comix proffered a form perfect for self-examination and analysis, echoing the notion that the 'personal is political'" (271). As the chapters in this book demonstrate, self-examination, political discourse, and the connections between the personal and the political are all prominent aspects of Claremont's writing style. Each of the scholars listed above, however, locates this relationship between second-wave feminism and comics within the underground comix scene of the 1970s, not within the comics of mainstream publishers like Marvel. Thus, Claremont's adoption and mobilization of second-wave feminist ideas for his stories may not have been unprecedented in the medium, but these ideas were certainly less prominent (if identifiable at all) in the comics mainstream.

Claremont's approach to female characters clearly shows the influence of key historical and political movements of the era, but his lived experience may have had the greater impact. Indeed, when asked in interviews about where his strong female characters come from, his first response was usually to talk about his mother.

> My mom, when she was in college, ended up joining the RAF because she wanted to be a fighter pilot. They wouldn't let her be one because women aren't allowed to fly Spitfires. So she ended up serving on a radar station on the south coast of Britain in 1940, which was an extremely adventurous time to be in that place, doing that job. So I figure if I know people who do this for real, why can't I put their equivalent on paper? Why should women in comics just be girlfriends? Why can't there be boyfriends? Why can't you create idiosyncratic individuals and then put them through hell? No one else was doing it, I figured, "The heck? I'll take a shot and see what happens." (*Marvel's Behind the Mask* n.p.)

Translating the heroism of his mother to the page thus became an important aspect of Claremont's approach to writing female characters, but also sparked a desire, as he mentions above, to redress what he describes as a conspicuous absence of strong female characters in superhero comics of the time.

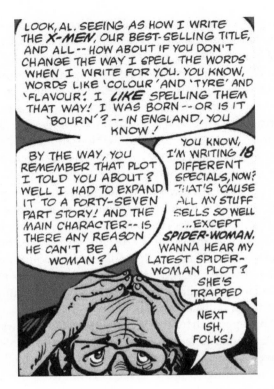

**Fig. 0.2.** *References to Claremont's approach to female characters in* Editori-Al *(Marvel Fanfare, vol. 1, no. 2) and* Johnny We Hardly Knew Ye *(Strikeforce: Morituri, vol. 1, no. 13).*

Claremont's mantra "Is there any reason this character can't be a woman?" is so famous that it appears at least twice *within* Marvel comics of the era, showing up in both *Marvel Fanfare* no. 2 (Milgrom) and *Strikeforce: Morituri* no. 13 (Gillis) (fig. 0.2). Claremont's commitment to progressive gender representation was—quite literally—a joke to other Marvel writers, one that saw international publication.

Claremont's deployment of women in diverse roles aligns particularly well with the central thesis of Betty Friedan's book *The Feminine Mystique* (arguably the most pivotal text in the cultivation of second-wave feminism in America).[3] Friedan posits that for women, identity has been falsely entangled with the concept of domestic servitude, and they have been excluded from roles outside of the home. By building a fantasy world in which women occupy nondomestic roles (ranging from airline pilot to team leader for a mutant superhero group), Claremont's portrayal of female characters expanded the number of roles available to women in comics of the era.

Also at play in this historical period was the growing awareness of internal divisions in feminism and the various ways that other social categories were being decentralized within the movement. This is something explored by Sabrina Alimahomed in "Thinking Outside the Rainbow: Women of Color Redefining Queer Politics and Identity," a historical survey in which she argues that the civil rights movement, the women's rights movement, and the gay rights movement of the 1960s and 1970s all featured myopic views of how different forms of oppression impacted constituencies.

> Women of color who were involved in the progressive movements of the 1960s and 1970s (e.g., the feminist movement, or the Civil Rights movement) pointed to the ways they experienced multiple oppressions simultaneously, contrary to the experiences of white women and men of color, for whom race or gender was often their primary and only concern. (152)

In the eyes of Alimahomed, it was this era that exposed the fundamental need for intersectional consideration in feminist movements. In this light, Claremont's character Storm again becomes a pivotal tool for the ongoing advancement of feminist aims of the period, simply for intersecting race, sexuality, gender, and class in all the ways that she does and, by extension, examining the impact that those intersections have on contrasting the social categories surrounding the other characters within the group dynamic of the X-Men, including the heterosexual, white male characters.

As we turn our attention to the portrayal of male-identified superheroes, we find that Claremont's run on *UXM* shows certain patterns and character arcs with the potential to interrogate and undermine the concept of hegemonic masculinity. Claremont's main approach to this task is to undertake a broad and parallax exploration of sex and gender roles in terms of their impact on individual characters.

In *Masculinities*, R. W. Connell defines sex roles as "a man or a woman ... enacting a *general* set of expectations which are attached to one's sex" (22). Connell perceives these roles as mutually dependent: "In this approach there are always two sex roles in any cultural context, a male one and a female one. Masculinity and femininity are quite easily interpreted as internalized sex roles, the products of social learning or 'socialization'" (22). For Connell, this approach is a culturally constructed fallacy (in line with earlier theories of constructionist feminism), but for Claremont-era *X-Men* readers, the idea of strict gender roles had very much pervaded the culture, and the notion that society was split into two sexes with culturally defined attributes and tendencies was well entrenched.

Although Connell uses the term *sex role*, it has been commonly replaced by the term *gender role* in modern parlance, with *sex role* now referring more to one's role in sexual interactions than the gender identity assigned to an individual at birth. (Also, *sex role* is not to be confused with *sex categories*, the term preferred by Patrick Hogan in *Sexual Identities* to refer to the categories by which biological sex is culturally defined.) For my part, I use both terms as needed. Regardless of semantics, these roles form what Julie Rivkin and Michael Ryan identify as "codes of conformity" in which masculinity and femininity become far extremes on a spectrum of gender performance: "Women can be just as much 'masculine' as men, and biological men might simply be 'masculine' (or pretend to be such) only out of obedience to cultural codes" (530). Simply put, sex may be biological (though by no means binary), but gender is performative. It has to be noted, however, that in Marvel comics of the 1970s and 1980s, sex and gender performance were very closely allied to a problematic degree and most often binary in nature—hence the merit of using the single-axis approach as the starting point for discussions of gender in this project.

Even something like Bechdel testing risks affirming the cultural myth that gender is binary. This is not my ambition. The Bechdel test works on Claremont's sample because the world of gender identity depicted at the behest of the Marvel Publishing Group and under the watchful eye of the Comics Code Authority is indeed binary in nature, and, as my analysis will demonstrate, it is only through subversive means that Claremont is able to portray gender deviancy. My approach, then, draws from that of Hortense Spillers, who defends the practice of analyzing the male/female Imaginary (capitalized in accordance with Lacan's usage of the term) in literature as follows:

> At a time when current critical discourses appear to compel us more and more decidedly toward gender "undecidability," it would appear reactionary, if not dumb, to insist on the integrity of female/male gender. But undressing these conflations of meaning, as they appear under the rule of dominance, would restore, as figurative possibility, not only Power to the Female (for Maternity), but also power to the Male (for Paternity). (66)

Thus, by studying the articulation of gender as binary in the universe of Marvel comics, we can come to understand its politics and rhetoric alongside Claremont's contribution to the broader cultural undermining of this Imaginary, a contribution that includes a variety of important intersections with these prescribed gender roles.

As I will demonstrate, one of the great strengths of the Claremont run is the broader cosmology of male and female characters it presents, and the various ways that identity markers such as race, nationality, religion, age, class, and sexuality intersect with each character's gender performance. Indeed, the interrogation of those relationships—something that is deeply important to Claremont's characterization of each individual superhero—will form a major component of every reading of character that this study undertakes. Claremont's work explores intersections with other social categories in order to explore what Grzanka, in his discussion of the power of intersectionality, refers to as "interventions and interruptions in hegemonic knowledge production" (xxii). By portraying characters whose momentum and trajectory along character arcs are defined by intersecting social categories rather than by the single-axis variable of gender, Claremont's characters hold the potential to undermine the very concept of fixed gender roles. Grzanka further argues that intersectionality can reveal to us that "no objectivity is total, and all knowledge is partial" (xxiii). Thus Claremont's writing might produce a view of gender that is not totalizing but instead embraces partiality—and with it, consideration for empirical structures and strictures that inform the concept of the gender role.

As already mentioned, those gender roles have tremendous presence in both the comics of Claremont's era and (relatedly) in the popular consciousness of the time. A simple example would be Connell's argument that the masculine sex role contains a greater affordance for violence and aggression compared to the feminine sex role (xx). This concept has been readily identified in comics, specifically by scholars such as Carol Cooper, who describes it as follows:

> Sue and Marvel Girl were still expected to use their softer, less flashy powers in more defensive strategies than their male teammates. Female villains might be allowed to "fight dirty," as it were, but such unladylike behaviour was presumed evil, and, as such, couldn't be part of the superheroine's repertoire. (186)

There's an important intersection of sex and heroism here, one that is also articulated by Richard Reynolds in *Super Heroes: A Modern Mythology*, but the greater point is that despite the fantasy trappings of the superhero narrative, it is by no means immune to drawing on and perpetuating traditional gender roles. Indeed, superhero comics might be an influential site for the recapitulation of gender roles.

In pursuit of quantifiable data on this subject, and building on the previous work of scholars such as Carolyn Cocca and Lillian S. Robinson, I isolated specific comics tropes that tend to reify gender roles and coded them in our content analysis. With the aid of my research assistants, we then went through the entire Claremont run, issue by issue, to see which gender roles Claremont's work supports and which it undermines.

As an example, our study analyzed the instances of X-Men's clothing being torn, X-Men being tortured, and X-Men losing their superpowers.[4] These are all ways in which female characters are frequently sexualized or objectified in North American comics. Claremont's numbers move against that a little bit. His male X-Men have their clothing torn just as often as female characters do (sixty-one male instances vs. sixty female). His male X-Men are tortured almost as often as his female X-Men are (eight male instances vs. six female), and his male characters lose their superpowers far more often than his female characters do (fifty-seven male instances vs. thirty-one female).

Heterosexual white masculinity is also problematically associated with a lack of emotional expression (Connell 131–133). But in the Claremont run we again have data to support a subversion of this gender role. Noncombative physical contact (typically an expression of affection) is exhibited by all of the prominent male characters, as well as the female ones (fig. 0.3). The X-Men's alpha male leader, Cyclops, in particular, does

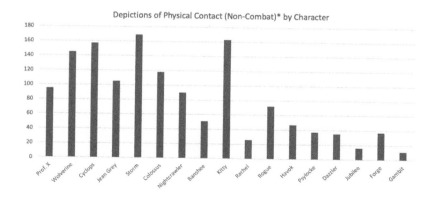

**Fig. 0.3.** *Physical contact data for each Claremont* X-Men *character.*

a lot of hugging, kissing, and hand-holding despite being largely absent in the back half of the Claremont run (for reasons taken up in chapter 4).

Additionally, the male X-Men participate in the romantic melodramas of the text to a larger degree than might be expected within the superhero genre. As Darowski notes, "Claremont's writing style has been called soap operatic because of its reliance on fluctuating romantic pairings, interpersonal tension between team members, and subplots" (*X-Men* 60). Historically, this did indeed create friction with *UXM*'s readers at the outset of the run. Media-studies scholar Miles Booy notes how the *X-Men* fan base would insultingly compare the series to daytime soap operas:

> The disparaging comparison to the culturally denigrated form of the soap opera and the accusation of characters' "hand-wringing" were criticisms which Claremont's overt emotionalism made easy. Doubts about one's ability to fully contribute to (or lead) the team, concern for other members, questioning the morality of pragmatic actions and indecision over romantic feelings were common across the team. Storm had claustrophobia to contend with, and Colossus bouts of homesickness. (49)

Simply put, the fans noticed a change in *X-Men* comics when Claremont came aboard as the writer, and his depiction of emotionally vulnerable characters was not always welcomed, at least not at the outset.

The total of on-panel kisses featuring male X-Men is seventy-nine, compared to fifty-one featuring females; thirteen male dates are depicted,

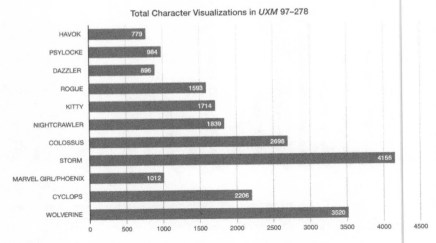

**Fig. 0.4.** *Total on-panel images of each Claremont* X-Men *character.*

compared to five female dates; and thirty-seven male expressions of the words "I love you" are uttered, compared to twenty-five female expressions of the phrase.

We can also look at the more basic elements of representation in the form of simple presence and prominence. We might, for example, expect a comic book to foreground the male characters at the expense of the female ones. Again, however, we find that this is not the case in Claremont's work, as evidenced by the total number of drawings of each character throughout the run (fig. 0.4). There are all manner of competing variables here, but in concert with the qualitative analysis still to come in this chapter, and with the findings of the other data sets, a pattern emerges.

Now, of course, we might argue that the above graph does little to reflect quality of representation, since female characters may often be illustrated ornamentally, without having an active role in the story.[5] However, in terms of interior monologue and perspective, the data again does not suggest a privileging of the male perspective. The female character Storm, for example, has twice as many thought bubbles as any other *X-Men* character in the entirety of the run, and Kitty Pryde has the second most. The alpha male characters Wolverine and Cyclops have the third and fourth most thought bubbles.

Interior perspective and agency can still be different things, but comics scholarship (drawing largely from broader media studies) has cultivated some useful analytical theories for broaching the subject of sexualization.

Though outdated, heteronormative, and essentialist, one such tool that is frequently invoked by comics studies comes from film theorist Laura Mulvey, who famously defines the rhetoric of the male gaze.

Building on foundational work by Sigmund Freud, Mulvey establishes how representing women as sex objects in film serves to reinforce patriarchal hierarchies in Western culture: "Unchallenged, mainstream film coded the erotic into the language of the dominant patriarchal order" (16). She suggests that this process works by either demystifying the represented woman or by fetishizing her.[6] In order to demystify, cinema invites voyeurism. The audience is made to see the represented female in her most private and personal spaces. Accordingly, she is completely ignorant of the audience's presence. The voyeuristic perspective that film endorses thus exposes all the mysteries that the object of male affection may potentially withhold. Through surveillance, the male audience member holds total power over the highly exposed female object. Furthermore, because the audience is invited to watch the film (this being the basic purpose of the film—to be seen), the film endorses voyeurism and normalizes this aspect of visual pleasure as something that is socially acceptable.

Fetishism, for Mulvey, occurs when the staging of the film leads the male audience member to perceive the female character as no more than an object of fantasy.

> The determining male gaze projects its fantasy onto the female figure, which is styled accordingly. In their traditional exhibitionist role women are simultaneously looked at and displayed, with their appearance coded for strong visual and erotic impact so that they can be said to connote *to-be-looked-at-ness*. (19)

The female characters are used for spectacle to such an extent that the diegesis of the film is often broken and simply functions as a framing mechanism to justify the spectacle of the woman. As Mulvey notes, "Fetishistic scopophilia builds up the physical beauty of the object, transforming it into something satisfying in itself" (21). The objectified female provides the pleasure of looking for the male audience member. That is her function, even at the expense of verisimilitude or the illusion of the fourth wall.[7]

In comics, an emphasis on visual pleasure is common practice. From the first comic books/periodicals in the 1920s and 1930s, comics have maintained a tradition of exhibiting women in a manner that is inherently fetishistic, voyeuristic, and sexist. Comics scholar Scott Bukatman summarizes the situation quite effectively:

The spectacle of the female body in these titles is so insistent, and the fetishism of breasts, thighs, and hair is so complete, that the comics seem to dare you to say anything about them that isn't just redundant. *Of course*, the female form has absurdly exaggerated sexual characteristics; *of course*, the costumes are skimpier than one could (or should) imagine; *of course*, there's no visible way that these costumes could stay in place; *of course*, these women represent simple adolescent masturbatory fantasies (with a healthy taste of the dominatrix). (65)

These tropes are not just obvious, they are also deeply entrenched and self-perpetuating, even in the face of opposition.

This fixity is evident in the superhero genre's exaggerated representations of gender norms, and in the related fact that when sexuality is explicitly present in mainstream superhero texts, it is often at the expense of female characters. The hypersexualization of female characters in superhero texts is so pervasive that publicly critiquing it has been known to provoke rape and death threats. (Bukatman 63)

These two observations are both focused on visual representation, but Claremont was writing *X-Men* comics for sixteen years, never drawing them. True-to-form *X-Men* comics were not immune to the visual fetishism that Bukatman mentions, but similar to scholar Susan Kerns's reading of *Tank Girl* as a multidimensional text that supports both the male gaze and female reader identification, we might argue that the male gaze aspects of *X-Men* comics were accompanied by an implicit acknowledgment of female readers through the portrayal of strong, self-aware female characters. Moreover, when analyzing a scribe such as Claremont, our interest lies more in what the characters say and do than on how they look while doing it. Indeed, with Claremont's X-Women we often find a compelling character underneath the visual fantasy, even when placed in situations that created opportunities to illustrate a sexual spectacle. This is more than can be said about many comics whose female characters seem to exist solely for the sake of appealing to the male gaze as outlined by Mulvey.

This interest in character agency also aligns with the thesis of what is perhaps the most famous essay on the subject of narrative gender roles for women in comics, Gloria Steinem's introduction to the edited volume *Wonder Woman* (1972), in which she writes,

The trouble is that the comic book performers of such superhuman feats—and even of dimly competent ones—are almost always heroes. Literally. The female child is left to believe that, even when her body is as grown-up as her spirit, she will still be in the childlike role of helping with minor tasks, appreciating men's accomplishments, and being so incompetent and passive that she can only hope some man can come to her rescue. . . . But dependency and zero accomplishments get very dull as a steady diet. The only option for a girl reader is to identify with the male characters—pretty difficult, even in the androgynous years of childhood. If she can't do that, she faces limited prospects: an "ideal" life of sitting around like a Technicolor clothes horse, getting into jams with villains, and saying things like "oh, Superman! I'll always be grateful to you," even as her hero goes off to bigger and better adventures. It hardly seems worth learning to tie our shoes. (2)

In essence, Steinem is calling for narrative agency, the capacity for female characters to drive or impact the story, rather than simply being impacted by it.

As the next few chapters articulate, during the Claremont run the X-Women achieved a rare amount of agency. Claremont defied convention by building his first major story arc around Jean Grey, a character who had previously aligned directly with the trope of the token female character on a superhero team. Thereafter, Storm is the driving force of the run. In addition to having her be both the leader of the team and the most prominently featured character, Claremont frequently utilized Storm as a viewpoint character, someone whose internal thought processes the reader is made to inhabit, and thus the main reader surrogate through whom the events of the series are experienced.

On the other side of the hero/villain binary, we should note that the most famous villain in the Claremont run is also a woman: the Dark Phoenix, whose power, menace, and resonance equal or exceed that of any male *X-Men* villain. But our data also shows that Claremont's most frequently appearing villain is Mystique, another female character.

These same characters with narrative agency also demonstrate a poignant deviation from the norm of superheroine power sets. As Cooper has noted, superheroines typically have nonphysical power sets, but Claremont challenges this by establishing Storm as the powerhouse of the team, Rogue as a gritty brawler, Kitty and Psylocke as ninja warriors, and, of course, Jean Grey, the meek girl next door who often sat on the sidelines during the pre-Claremont run, as a world-altering goddess.

Finally, on the subject of overarching gender representation, we need to consider the role of scope in Claremont's portrayal of gender. There are two ways to approach this task. The first is to consider the sheer size of the run and the extent to which Claremont was not just allowed to evolve, but encouraged or even required to do so. What makes his work so unique is the sample size—the length of the run and the subsequent vastness of his characterizations.

This leads to the question of scope: not the number of issues or years that Claremont had to work with, but the sheer number of characters and how that diverse roster articulates a broad perspective on gender roles. Carolyn Cocca specifically singles this aspect out as perhaps the most remarkable attribute of Claremont's portrayal of women, noting that "these characters' looks, powers, motivations, and personalities display a range of characterizations of girls and women whose centrality and diversity can provide points of entry, identification, and empathy for a wide spectrum of comic readers" (121). Cocca's point here is pivotal. *X-Men*, under Claremont, wasn't just female friendly; it was friendly to a wide swathe of different types of people embodying or practicing a wide spectrum (a galaxy, really) of different gender roles. For his part, Ramzi Fawaz refers to the X-Women as a "feminist cosmology" (149).

Though atypical of superhero team books at the time, Claremont's cultivation of this cosmology of different female characters does potentially reflect key developments of feminist discourse from this time period. Marilyn Friedman, for example, notes how "some feminists in the 1980s began recommending a relational concept of autonomy, one that treats social relationships and human community as central to the realization of autonomy" (40). She argues that mainstream accounts of feminine autonomy have "neglected the possibilities for autonomy available in women's traditional relational practices" (58). By building a coalition of female characters with different backgrounds, identity markers, and complex interrelationships with each other, Claremont uses relational practice to cultivate a broader and more diverse representation of feminine agency through community. Both Cocca (125) and Margaret Galvan (49) identify this theme of feminine coalition as an important emergent property of *X-Men* comics under Claremont.

Simply by moving from a single token female character to a full feminine cosmology in which women relate to both men and to other women creates a representational affordance that other comics could not achieve.

This is especially important from the perspective of intersectional feminism, with female characters in *UXM* uniting and supporting each other not just because of gender affinity, but also across other boundaries such as race, religion, class, and age. Fawaz, for example, speaks to the importance of the communal bond between the white X-Woman Jean Grey and the black X-Woman Ororo Munroe (380), and Galvan speaks to the importance of the Ororo/Kitty relationship in transgressing age barriers (49). Taking all of this as a starting point, we can begin to isolate key characters in *UXM* in order to explicate their individual relationships to gender roles and how these individual sites of gender deviance operate within the broader cosmology that the series creates.

Chapter 1 of this book builds on the robust existing scholarship on the subject of X-Woman Jean Grey/Phoenix and integrates it into the figure of "the Claremont Woman," known within the Marvel bullpen as "any kind of woman who, at the drop of a hat, will machine-gun the hell out of anyone in her way" (Powell 16). By connecting Jean to Moira MacTaggert (the human-among-mutants character in the series), I establish Claremont's foundational portrayal of feminine agency in the run.

Chapter 2 frames the Ororo/Storm relationship as both the centerpiece of Claremont's run on *X-Men* and the centerpiece of his evolving articulation of nonnormative gender behavior in *X-Men* comics, with a particular emphasis on intersectional feminism. Storm is both the first woman to lead a Marvel superhero team and the first black character to lead a Marvel superhero team. Her character undergoes the starkest, and most literal, transformation of gender identity, shifting from projecting stereotypes of maternity, nurturing, and passive sexuality to a character with resolve, agency, and libido around which the evolution of the entire series ultimately pivots, a process that is deeply embroiled in the concept of cultural repatriation and sexual exploration.

Chapter 3 explores the complex spectrum of gender deviancy presented by Claremont's second generation of female characters, with particular emphasis on the Betsy Braddock/Psylocke character's intersectional dialogue with Lacan's concept of the feminine masquerade and the extent to which the character expresses femininity ironically. I also present a close reading of the Alison Blaire/Dazzler character's self-critical exploration of toxic masculinity in an issue titled *Star 90*, which articulates a subversive portrayal of the casual dismissal of man-on-woman violence in popular culture. Finally, I close out the chapter with a look at an issue titled *Ladies Night*, a deeply ironic story featuring X-Women performing femininity in directly satiric ways.

With chapter 4, I transition to Claremont's male-identified characters. I explore how the character of Scott Summers/Cyclops personifies broader cultural anxieties about paradigmatic shifts in patriarchal culture in direct response to second-wave feminism. Cyclops is the alpha male leader of the team and an emblem of 1970s white, heterosexual, middle American masculinity, but he becomes anxious and threatened when his girlfriend, Jean, achieves a previously unfathomable level of power. How Cyclops negotiates his agency within both the relationship dynamic and the leadership hierarchy of the X-Men symbolizes broader cultural paradigm shifts and gives voice to the specific anxieties that they create. At the same time, Cyclops progressively becomes a masculinist hero with a rare level of dawning self-perception about the ways in which hegemonic masculinity and privilege have distanced him from his own self-actualization.

Chapter 5 connects the most famous X-Man, Logan/Wolverine, to other archetypes of pop culture masculinity, specifically the cowboy (an emblem of white American masculinity) and the samurai (an emblem of Japanese masculinity). My argument here is that Logan/Wolverine is uniquely capable of undermining hegemonic masculinity due to his broader entrenchment within it. He is a hypermasculine character who is constantly at odds with those hypermasculine traits. Through a close reading of the issues titled *Wolverine: Alone!* and *Wounded Wolf*, I establish a trajectory of progressive gender deviance as, essentially, Wolverine's counterintuitive character arc within the series as a whole.

Chapter 6 starts with Kurt Wagner/Nightcrawler's refractive portrayal of masculinity in juxtaposition with that of Wolverine, his best friend. From there, I explore the emergence of the female gaze in response to Nightcrawler before transitioning to discuss Alex Summers/Havok, whose performance of symbolic emasculation holds the potential to undermine the implied connection between the superhero role itself and the masculine ideal. I close with a reading of *Men!*, Claremont's equally satiric follow-up to *Ladies Night*.

For the conclusion, I draw in Bart Beaty and Benjamin Woo's configuration of cultural capital in order to establish the scope and scale of Claremont's influence in popular culture and the unique position of prominence occupied by his work, all with the ultimate goal of determining the range of Claremont's ideas about gender and projecting a trajectory for the future of Claremont studies.

CHAPTER 1

# Jean, Moira, and the Archetypal "Claremont Woman"

Here was a nice, normal girl from exurban New York, late teens or barely twenty, upper-middle class, educated North American instantly gaining the capability to stand higher in the Cosmic standings than the celestials. For her, literally, there was no division between conception (or desire) and reality.

–CHRIS CLAREMONT, INTRODUCTION TO *MARVEL MASTERWORKS: THE UNCANNY X-MEN*, VOL. 5

One of Claremont's first original *X-Men* character creations, the scientist Moira MacTaggert, helped coin the term "Claremont Woman" by, quite literally, entering the comics world guns blazing. This term, frequently passed around the Marvel bullpen and among comics creators in general, is defined by the author himself as "any kind of woman who, at the drop of a hat, will machine-gun the hell out of anyone in her way" (qtd. in Powell 16).[1] While this might sound like an unrealistic or even irresponsible portrayal, many male characters serve as power fantasies in comics, and very much demonstrate the same principles in ways that conform to media portrayals of hegemonic masculinity.

As the torchbearer for the term Claremont Woman, Moira Mac-Taggert is an excellent first subject to explore. She is introduced to the reader in *UXM* no. 96. Her first line (a response to a male character's impatience) is "Ah beg yuir pardon! Mah name is Moira MacTaggert an' ah've been engaged as a housekeeper here by Professor Charles Xavier. D'you want to make somethin' of it, then?!" (*Night of the Demon!* 6). A scene later, the mansion is attacked by a demon. Moira is soon thereafter seen emerging from the armory with an M-16 assault rifle, spraying bullets at the demon while she remarks, "Let's see how yon kelpie fares against close-range machine gun fire!" (15). Despite being identified as a housekeeper (a domestic and traditionally feminine role in media portrayals), Moira is presented as a character who deviates from type.

This characterization will prove even more apt in later issues, which reveal that the housekeeper role was a ruse by Xavier/Professor X, and Moira has actually been a silent partner in the formation of the X-Men since long before the team was even formed. Instead of their house-keeper, she is, in fact, the world's leading expert on mutation, other than Xavier himself. Here Moira is elevated to the role of prestigious scientist, a Nobel Prize winner at a time when only seventeen women had received that honor in real life, just seven of them in the STEM fields, and at a time when that field was considered predominantly masculine. In 1976, "women represented only 7.5% of the faculty in physical sciences and less than 1% in engineering" (Dearman and Plisko 355). Her chosen discipline, then, forms an interesting intersection with her gender portrayal, creating a sharp contrast with the earlier role of housekeeper.

Moira's scientific background is no novelty either. Claremont frequently constructed narratives around her scientific inquiries, portraying her efforts (and accomplishments) with both gravitas and nobility. In *UXM* no. 125, we get a technophilic visualization of Moira in her lab, wearing a futuristic jumpsuit and goggles, alongside the narration: "This is Dr. Moira MacTaggert—second only to Charles Xavier as an authority on genetic mutation. She's Scots—a highlander born and bred—and she doesn't scare easily" (*There's Something Awful on Muir Island!* 2). Here the juxtaposition of dramatic prose with a technophilic image can lend the scene a tone of severity and heroism. Moira's work is portrayed as a noble effort to help people, one that involves courage, will, and sacrifice.

From a cultural perspective, Moira is also at odds with a perceived stereotype about women in science fiction (SF). In her highly influential 1975 essay "American SF and the Other," Ursula Le Guin notes,

> The women's movement has made most of us conscious of the fact that SF has either totally ignored women, or presented them as squeaking dolls subject to instant rape by monsters—or old-maid scientists de-sexed by hypertrophy of the intellectual organs—or, at best, loyal little wives or mistresses of accomplished heroes. (97)

As a narrative built around the concept of genetic mutation, *X-Men* comics can be classified as SF, but Moira does not easily fit into any of the boxes that Le Guin argues SF has confined female characters within. Though a scientist, that identity marker does not confine Moira to the old-maid performance of femininity that Le Guin suggests SF forces upon female scientists. We can see this through Dave Cockrum's physical portrayal of Moira and through the immediate attraction that the X-Man Banshee (serving as a reader surrogate) demonstrates upon first meeting her (fig. 1.1). She is not de-sexed for being a scientist. Indeed, her intellect, cool rationality, and pragmatism can all be said to contribute to her appeal.

**Fig. 1.1.** *Moira MacTaggert arrives at the X-Mansion in* Night of the Demon! *(UXM, vol. 1, no. 96). Dave Cockrum, penciler.*

This is the starting point for the portrayal of Moira in her most prominent story arc, the *Proteus Saga*, which revolves around her past relationships and the consequences of the choices she made. Here, Moira prominently takes the traditionally masculine scientist role and pairs it with a maternal role when it is revealed that her son is Proteus, a mutant with awe-inspiring power. Proteus has been contained at Moira's Muir Island laboratory for most of his life, but he escapes in a freak accident and begins to terrorize the surrounding villages, killing people and stealing their bodies. The conflict that unfolds thus offers the potential to place Moira into a nurturer role by focusing on her maternal responsibility, but Claremont's story accomplishes quite the opposite.

As the story unfolds, it is Moira who understands and accepts, better than anyone, that Proteus needs to die. When the X-Men's field leader, Cyclops, hesitates to allow the use of lethal force in pursuit of her son, Moira knocks him out, explaining, "I'm not playin' by your rules, Scott, not this time. And I can't afford the time to argue or explain. Thanks to your interference, it may already be too late!" (*The Quality of Hatred* 6). With that, she walks off with a rifle to find and take care of her wayward son.

The trail leads to Moira's former husband, who we learn was abusive. She confronts him boldly. When he becomes angry at the news that he has a son he never knew about, she draws a pistol. The two-panel sequence makes it clear that she is not the one retreating. He is. She informs him,

"Not a move, not a word, not even a sound, Joe—or I'll do now what I so desperately wanted to do twenty years ago." On her way out of the encounter, Moira thinks to herself, "I loved the boy, Joe. I tried to teach him to love, to care, to be kind—but all he saw was the pain you'd caused—an' the hatred I felt for you, eatin' away at my soul like a maggot" (19). This tenacity of character amidst emotionally harrowing circumstances extends throughout the remainder of the storyline, which sees Moira courageously pursuing her own son up to the point of his inevitable destruction. Only in the instant *after* he falls—killed in battle by the superhero Colossus—does she allow herself to feel the full emotional weight of her decisions, finally breaking down and seeking comfort in her friends.

Although Moira sets an important standard for Claremont's portrayal of female characters, she is not technically an X-Woman, nor is she consistently a central character in the narrative. In fact, Moira is absent from more issues than she appears in throughout the Claremont run. When he first came on board as the writer of *UXM*, Claremont inherited a team that had only one female *X-Men* character, Storm. Storm merits greater attention for her depiction of gender roles in dialogue with any number of intersections, but I would first like to speak about Jean Grey as a legacy character with a highly gendered history that Claremont consciously subverts in the pages of *UXM*.

Jean Grey was one of the original *X-Men* characters created by Stan Lee and Jack Kirby in 1963. She is a cisgender, heterosexual, white all-American woman from a well-to-do upbringing in an upper-middle-class suburb. Though she leaves the team in Claremont's first issue (which was plotted by a different writer), she quickly finds herself sucked back into the story just three issues later when she is abducted by Sentinels (giant anti-mutant robots). She is then rescued by a team of X-Men whom she herself then rescues by risking her life to pilot them back to earth in an unsafe spaceship that only she can fly (*Greater Love Hath No X-Man* [*UXM* no. 100]).

In his first move after taking over Jean, a longstanding character, Claremont eliminated her condescending, gendered code name, Marvel Girl, which she had held for a decade (despite being an adult at this point). By issue no. 101, Marvel Girl was no more. Jean Grey, transformed by an encounter with a mysterious cosmic entity during a near-death experience piloting the spaceship, bursts forth from the sunken wreckage of the ship proclaiming, "Hear me, X-Men. No longer am I the woman you knew. I am fire! And life incarnate! Now and forever—I am Phoenix!" (*Like a Phoenix, from the Ashes* 7). This dramatic entrance would set the tone for the broader nature of Jean's transformation from a timid sideline character to a world-altering goddess with seemingly limitless power.

For Miles Booy, the Phoenix transformation is well in keeping with Claremont's broader pattern of gender representation.

> This revamping of Jean's character was part of Claremont's tendency to write female characters that were as strong and as powerful as the male ones. In keeping with this, Claremont rejected the common tradition of giving hero(ine)s gender-specific code names (Spider-Man, Wonder Woman, etc.), preferring instead to follow the alternative practice of using gender-neutral identities. (36)

Jason Powell echoes this sentiment in his own book, calling Phoenix an early example of Claremont's "feminist sensibilities" (25). The reconfiguration of an iconic character is a dramatic way to start a run, but it can set the tone regarding those same sensibilities from the outset.

Once transformed, Jean (now Phoenix) is the subject of an ambitious and extensive story arc that culminates with her self-destruction in the *Dark Phoenix Saga*. There are a number of asides that occur, but if we perceive the *Dark Phoenix Saga* as directly connected to Jean's initial transformation into Phoenix (thus viewing this period as one collective story arc), then the broader Phoenix/Dark Phoenix saga is roughly forty issues long, unfolding over the course of four years in an unusually cohesive and non-episodic manner (by the standards of the time). Simply put, Claremont built a massive and ambitious storyline around a female character, giving Jean/Phoenix a spotlight and platform that had traditionally been denied to the character, as well as most female characters in Marvel comics up to that time.

During this story arc, Phoenix is portrayed as the powerhouse of the team, frequently shocking the other members with the extent of her abilities. She does this in defiance of, at times, her own publisher. Dave Cockrum, who co-created Phoenix, recalled in an interview how Marvel editor-in-chief Jim Shooter expressed disdain at the very concept of the super-empowered Jean Grey. When asked why Shooter wanted to get rid of Phoenix, Cockrum said, "Shooter hated strong female characters. When we first introduced Phoenix, we wanted her to fight Thor or the Silver Surfer, but Shooter wouldn't allow it. He said no female is going to beat Thor or the Silver Surfer" (qtd. in DeFalco 91). Claremont cleverly got around this edict by having Phoenix square off instead with a character named Firelord who had previously defeated both Thor and the Silver Surfer. Phoenix wins (*Phoenix Unleashed!* 26).

Prior to Claremont's cultivation of Jean's agency, the character's main focus in the narrative revolved around her relationship to male characters on the team as potential love interests. At this point, Jean is in a relationship with Scott Summers (aka Cyclops), the alpha male of the team, a position he holds through three key attributes:

1. He is the team leader.
2. He is the favorite of Charles Xavier, their mentor and patriarch.
3. He is the victor of the hypermasculine rivalry for the affection of Jean Grey (a rivalry that briefly included Xavier himself).

Ignoring, for the moment, the pervasiveness of the third attribute as a sexist comics trope, my point is that when Claremont inherited the character, Cyclops was "the man" in a way that is perfectly consistent with established patterns of masculinity in comics by occupying the position of power, receiving the blessing of a patriarchal figure, and exhibiting dominance over other rivals for a woman's affection.

Within this context, however, Claremont was able to destabilize this entrenched pattern of masculine dominance through Jean. In the scene from *Greater Love Hath No X-Man* mentioned above, the damaged spaceship is about to crash, and Jean is the only one who can pilot it safely, though it might cost her life to do so. When Cyclops refuses to let her sacrifice herself, Jean's response is to take control. She refuses his order and even knocks him unconscious. She is insubordinate, thus renouncing his authority as both team leader and as her masculine partner. Jean further challenges gender roles here in openly opposing the hypermasculine Wolverine when he too attempts to stop her.

> The name is Jean, Mister—and I have just about had it with you! I have tried to like you, Wolverine—obnoxious little upstart that you are—but for the life of me, I don't know why I made the effort! So shut your mouth, and get into the life cell—now! Before I lose my temper! (*Greater Love Hath No X-Man* 30)

Faced with the fierceness of Jean's will, even the violently aggressive Wolverine backs down.

In future issues, Cyclops repeatedly expresses fear and insecurity over both how powerful Jean is and the nature of their relationship because she is meant to be his subordinate in his role as team leader, and as a woman in a relationship with a man (according to the established gender roles of the time).

These same anxieties culminate during their consummation scene in the *Dark Phoenix Saga*. I will take this scene up again in chapter 4 from the perspective of Cyclops's character, but for Jean's, the main thrust of the plot is as follows: Cyclops and teammate Angel are having a meeting on a remote mountaintop. Jean shows up with a picnic basket and blanket, at which point Angel, identifying her clear intent, states, "All of a sudden, I have the feeling I'm not wanted," to which Jean replies, "Perceptive lad. You'll go far." Angel flies away, leaving Scott and Jean alone. Jean immediately uses her Phoenix powers to transform her clothes into a revealing two-piece, saying, "We've all grown up, Scott"—an obvious double entendre given her choice of attire. Scott, uneasy about Jean's power, notes, "She did it again, changed from costume to street clothes by telekinetically rearranging the molecules of her outfit. Why do I find that so disconcerting? Why shouldn't Jean use her psi-powers to make her life easier?" (*And Hellfire Is Their Name!* 7). With the established sexual atmosphere of the scene, Scott's question may be read as reflective of his deeper anxieties about his subordinate status in their relationship.

From there, Jean takes control to an extreme degree. When Scott says that he has a lot on his mind, Jean issues a command: "Didn't you hear me?! It's time for a break! Stop being Cyclops, leader of the X-Men for awhile. Try being Scott Summers, lover of Jean Grey. Who knows, you might even enjoy yourself." To emphasize her point, she peels off Scott's visor (an important safety feature because Cyclops cannot control his optic blasts without it, and the blasts can be fatal). When he protests, she says, "Open your eyes, Scott. Nothing will happen. I'm telekinetically keeping your optic blasts in check. I . . . wanted to see your face, that's all. You have a good face." As she pulls him into her, he thinks, "I don't believe it! My eyes—How can Jean hold back all that power?!" before protesting aloud, "Jean . . ."—only to be interrupted by her again: "Hush. No questions now, my love. No words." The scene ends as they embrace in a passionate kiss (*And Hellfire Is Their Name!* 7).

In this instance, Jean asserts her sexual agency in the pursuit of her own pleasure, a pursuit that is often denied to women in popular media. As feminist philosopher Luce Irigaray (writing during this same approximate time period) notes, "[W]hat is most strictly forbidden to women today is that they should attempt to express their own pleasure" (77). This pursuit of pleasure is actually a major theme in the *Dark Phoenix Saga*. Darowski (*X-Men* 81) and Booy (43) both note that the language Jean uses, as well as the language Claremont uses to describe her, is the language of sexual desire. Claremont uses terms such as *ecstasy, hunger,* and *satisfaction*. In one interview he noted that even something as monstrous as her destruction of an inhabited planet is a sexual act for Jean. "To use a somewhat gross term, it was the quest for the cosmic orgasm. Her feeding . . . on the star was an act of love, of self-love, of masturbation probably" (qtd. in Booy 43). Thus, the Phoenix and Dark Phoenix sagas place emphasis on Jean's innately transgressive pursuit of her own sexual pleasure.

Jean Grey's sexual agency and control in her mountaintop encounter with Cyclops align quite effectively with scholarly readings of the sexual subtext in *X-Men* comics. Carol Cooper, for example, describes the presence of sexual sublimation in Claremont's *X-Men* as follows:

> With both secondary sex characteristics *and* mutant powers being triggered by adolescence, the new X-Men books [written by Claremont] contained built-in narrative reasons to examine how uncontrollable sexual urges and uncontrollable deployment of mutant powers might be linked. Learning to control new, shifting or suddenly erratic powers could easily be associated with repressing, sublimating or transferring sexual desire. (193)

Scott Bukatman's reading of sexual subtext in the series takes a similar angle. In discussing the mutant body of *UXM* comics, Bukatman describes how "erotic energies are sublimated into (other) bodily traumas, emissions and flows" (56), whereby Scott's optic blasts can be read as a form of symbolic sexual eruption—even ejaculation.

The bodily trauma that Scott suffered, which now necessitates the use of a visor, can thus be read as an important sexual symbol in itself—a tool by which his erotic energies are contained and controlled. Jean takes full control of that symbolical sexual eruption so that she can facilitate a literal one by bringing Scott to orgasm. She takes his sexuality and destroys its symbolic restraints while ushering him into literal, canonical sexuality, which in this scene might very well be Cyclops losing his virginity, a well-established rite of passage between adolescent and adult masculinity in the eyes of the culture of the time. Equally important, the long-awaited consummation of the Scott/Jean romance is enacted only once it is on Jean's terms entirely, an important contradiction of the existing performance of gender roles in Marvel comics of the era.

This reading is viable but subject to alternative perspectives and additional considerations. Scholar Sam Langsdale notes that "Because these overtly sexual acts take place after Jean's repressed desires surface . . . they, like Jean's power, take on the trappings of being out of control at best, and deadly at worst" (159). The pivot point might be in whether the reader perceives the sexual nature of this scene as the consummation of a long-standing romance or the seduction of a hero into corruption by an out-of-control heroine at the mercy of a malignant supernatural possession. Simply put, is Scott being seduced to commit a sin by an evil entity, or awakened to physical ecstasy by a long-desired partner?

Scott's anxiety in the consummation scene could support the sinful interpretation if the reader attributes his sense of dissonance and confusion to the looming emergence of Dark Phoenix. Jean will soon lose control over her Phoenix power and become a malevolent being bent on destruction. Indeed, it is quite possible to interpret *Dark Phoenix* as yet another story about a woman who cannot handle power, one that reifies the very idea that power itself is part of the masculine gender role, and that powerful women must be destroyed. As Langsdale notes, "Many feminist scholars and bloggers have critiqued the ways in which . . . [the *Dark Phoenix Saga*] links female desire and female sexuality with psychoses, lack of control, monstrosity and ultimately destruction" (153). However, in the *Dark Phoenix Saga*, it is Jean who ultimately destroys herself. In this light, readers could potentially interpret that action as a media-based assertion that women should internalize their subordination and destroy themselves in the face of power.[2]

On the other hand, it is not Jean's power that drives her mad (at least not in and of itself). In the buildup to the *Dark Phoenix Saga*, a malevolent masculine villain called Mastermind exploits a psychological vulnerability in Jean that might be read as the product of gender-based societal repression. With the assistance of the Hellfire Club (a cabal of wealthy superbeings pursuing global power through economic and political control), Mastermind manipulates Jean for months. He projects fantasies in her mind of the two of them together in a relationship that is openly sexual and sadistic, comingling her repressed fantasies of power and sex at a time when most of the X-Men are still expressing deep anxieties over the idea of Marvel Girl crossing the line from team accessory to a team member so powerful that it is often not apparent why she needs the team at all. This juxtaposition of Jean's good-girl life and bad-girl fantasies makes clear the dangers of repression. "Because Mastermind associated love with lust, violence and cruelty, that combination was the decadent cocktail he used to manipulate the Phoenix component of Jean's personality, for which every embodied sensation was an unprecedented and addictive thrill" (Cooper 194). Thus, the reading here suggests that society's repression of Jean's sexual agency (and, metaphorically, that of women in general) has made her vulnerable to manipulation.

The consequence of repression is the Dark Phoenix itself—the surfacing of Jean's id in a destructive way. Not only does the Dark Phoenix bring down ultimate destruction, but this transformation also strips the world of the tremendous benefit provided by the unmolested Phoenix, as established earlier in *Armageddon Now* (*UXM* no. 108). In that issue, Phoenix saves the universe by literally stitching reality together and is compared, in the prose narration that follows, to the Tiphareth from the Kabbalistic Tree of Life, a symbol of harmony and communion with the divine: "And the heart of the tree, the catalyst that binds these wayward souls together is Phoenix. Tiphareth. Child of the sun, child of life, the vision of the harmony of things" (30). The potential for good that Phoenix exhibits is even more impressive than the destructive power of Dark Phoenix, but the world loses that boon when Phoenix is pushed to the point of breaking.

We can also, however, read constructive (or creative) potential in the monstrosity of Dark Phoenix. Langsdale, for example, suggests that "Jean Grey/Phoenix be recognized as a model of Donna Harraway's 'promising monster'" (168), a figure with an emancipatory power similar to that of Harraway's famous cyborg construct, which spurred the field of cyborg feminism.

> Promising monsters are those who transgress borderlands, who demonstrate the porousness of boundaries, whose corporeality is not One, but undeniably bound up with text, myth, nature and the political. The promising monster is not one who asks, "Who am I?" but "Who are we?" (168)

This reading sees Dark Phoenix as an innately destabilizing force that transgresses and undermines boundaries of gender simply by calling so much attention to their social construction.

Even at the moment she decides to kill herself, Jean mentions that she might be able to control Phoenix, but she finds the prospect of eternal restraint unappealing: "Your way, I'd have to stay completely in control of myself every second of every day for the rest of my immortal life. If even one more person died at my hands. . . . It's better this way. Quick. Clean. Final" (*The Fate of the Phoenix!* 45). Comics scholar Mark D. White describes this as "the final expression of her autonomy, to make that choice" (35). He connects this action specifically to Kantian ethics, noting that "if, as Kant held, suicide is wrong because it sacrifices one's rationality and autonomy, then Jean's suicide can be seen as a way for her to save those faculties from being abused or sacrificed in a different way to the Phoenix

Force" (White 36). In this sense, Jean frees herself from patriarchal control and manipulation only by destroying herself outright.

The epilogue of the *Dark Phoenix Saga* comes up one page after Jean's suicide and is delivered by The Watcher, an omniscient, all-seeing being in Marvel continuity. He states: "The X-Men do not realize it—they may never accept it—but this day they have won perhaps the greatest victory of their young lives. Jean Grey could have lived to become a God. But it was more important to her that she die a human" (*The Fate of the Phoenix!* 46). Thus, the narrative itself establishes Jean's suicide as an act of autonomy and self-preservation.

Jean's death marks the end of Claremont's first major story arc in the pages of *UXM*. In it, he gave world-altering power to a woman, and all hell broke loose. This might not be a reflection of the danger of empowering women, however, but of the extent to which one woman in power can utterly and wholly disrupt, destabilize, and deconstruct an entire system from the inside out. That is, ironically, the exact role that Phoenix (as a character) may have played within the system of Marvel comics in this era.

CHAPTER 2

# Storm
## *From Mother-Goddess to Resolutely Indefinable*

> She is a little bit hard to get a handle on, because she is the leader of the group, and she has to be handled in a specific fashion that presented quite a challenge. She has a certain attitude that's tough to capture without dropping into clichés and certain poses. She's a character who's a little more complex than a Captain America who you have to draw in these star-spangled poses. She's not that cut and dried. She's got a little more complex and deeper personality. So it's kind of tough transferring her to a comic book. But that's probably one of the reasons I enjoy drawing her, because it's a bit of a challenge. But you have to be in the mood for that sort of thing. You have to have an unusual energy level the day you have to draw Storm.
>
> –MARC SILVESTRI, QUOTED IN FRED HEMBECK, *MARVEL AGE* NO. 69

Stating that one needs to understand Ororo Munroe/Storm in order to understand the portrayal of gender in *X-Men* comics is an uncontentious claim, but the larger claim articulated in this chapter is that one needs to understand Storm in order to understand *X-Men* comics—period. Though Wolverine became the most popular character in the franchise, Storm is both the most ubiquitous character in Chris Claremont's sixteen-year run as writer, and also the one around which the narrative is predominantly structured. This places her in a rare and unique position of prominence from which to unsettle the centralist perspectives on gender that historically dominated Marvel comics. But even as she advances key themes established by Moira and Jean, Storm achieves greater significance and complexity by entangling gender performance with social categories of religion, race, and sexuality. As bell hooks notes, "individuals who fight for the eradication of sexism without struggles to end racism or classism undermine their own efforts" (*Ain't I a Woman?* 12). Thus, the entanglements introduced by Storm's exploration of various social categories add both complexity and intersectionality to the broader exploration of gender roles in the series.

Ororo Munroe debuted in the first issue of *Giant-Size X-Men* in 1975.

This would be her only appearance in a comic book before Claremont came in as the main writer. She was co-created by Len Wein and Dave Cockrum, who gave her a simple backstory: Professor X travels to Kenya, where a weather-controlling mutant is being (mistakenly) worshipped as a goddess. He convinces her to join the X-Men in order to share her talents with the world. In Claremont's hands, she would quickly go from these humble origins to an important place in comics history while becoming the flagship character of the *X-Men* franchise at the height of its popularity.

As noted by scholar Rebecca Wanzo, "Comics creators have sometimes played on the distance between black bodies and models of ideal Americans, satirizing the impossibility of black bodies as representative of heroism or patriotism" (315). This is, arguably, the context in which Storm, as a character, rises to prominence as a major superhero in *X-Men* comics—against the grain of a tradition that saw her very existence as antithetical to the concept of the superhero.

As our data shows, the total number of Storm's interior monologues/thought bubbles is more than double that of any other character over the full course of the Claremont run. She is thus the most utilized viewpoint character of the series—the lens through which most of the key storylines, characters, and developments are perceived, reflected upon, and then contextualized within the broad continuity of Claremont's run. This emphasis on a woman's interior thoughts is atypical of a superhero team book in this era, but it also plays an important role in Storm's characterization as a black woman.

As Melissa Harris-Perry notes in her foreword to the anthology *Black Female Sexualities*, "the viewing public is most interested in seeing black women's bodies when they are subjected to ferocious terror" (ix). She is speaking to sexual exoticism in visual media here and identifies this trope as one of the key paradigms that black female sexuality tends to fall into. Erin D. Chapman picks this thread up in another chapter of that same anthology, suggesting that it is a lack of interior reflection on violence that perpetuates the bodies of black women as fodder for "rape fantasies" (142). As a member of a superhero team, Storm is subject to repeated instances of violence, including threats of sexual violence. Because her visual representation is coded for sexual appeal (discussed further below), it is therefore of pivotal importance that her perspective be the dominant one to avoid falling into this trope of black female sexuality.

Storm is also visualized more than any other character in the entirety of the Claremont run, appearing in 4,155 panels. Wolverine appears in 3,520 panels, the second highest total. Storm also appears on more covers than any other character in the run, a good indicator that she was successful

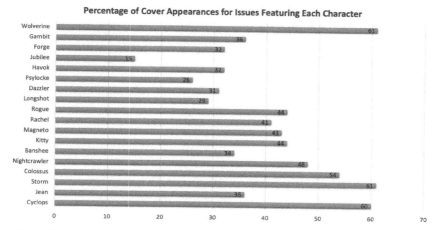

**Fig. 2.1.** *Percentage of cover appearances by* X-Men *character per issue featured.*

enough to merit representation on comics' most important piece of advertising. Thus, Storm is not just present in the narrative—she's a commodity as an intellectual property mobilized to help sell the narrative, appearing on 97 of 182 covers (53 percent), whereas Wolverine appears on 89 (49 percent). This, of course, means that Storm is the only character to appear on the majority of *UXM* covers during the Claremont run.

The most essential variable here is presence. Storm was on the team longer than any other *X-Men* character during the Claremont run, which obviously inflated her numbers compared to those of a character who appeared in only a dozen issues. To account for that variable, the same cover data is presented in figure 2.1 as an average of appearances, counting only the issues in which the character appears. Though Storm shares the spotlight here with the wildly popular Wolverine, she is still at the top of the chart, proving her tremendous presence in the series once again.

From a representational standpoint, presence can be a pivotal first step, and it is through presence that Storm achieves a number of significant comics milestones. She is the first African American leader of a Marvel superhero team, the first female leader of a Marvel superhero team, and "the most recognizable Black superhero in American popular culture" (carrington 91). She has also been acknowledged as "an early signifier of third wave feminism" (Campochiaro, "On X-(Wo)Men" n.p.).

Storm's representation did, however, fall into stereotype in the early issues of the Claremont run, where she shows some conformity to a sort of Josephine Baker-esque sexual exoticism (Deman, *Margins* 100–108) that sees her character align with existing stereotypes of black women that famously cater to the male gaze. Carolyn Cocca supports this interpretation, noting that Storm's introduction "is highly stereotyped" (125).

Carol Cooper, meanwhile, notes that "the first black X-Man somehow got cast as the mythic earth-mother/matriarch figure critiqued by many black feminists as both unrealistic and racist in its glib projection of inhuman perfection" (189). In these instances, scholars found that Storm was not particularly remarkable in the first issues of *X-Men* comics that she appeared in. Both scholars—indeed, perhaps all scholars on the subject of Storm—concede, however, that she got a great deal better from there. As Deborah Whaley notes, "Storm's metamorphosis over the years represents a visionary social subject that propels social change" (107). Whaley is mindful of the representational burden that Storm carries as a black woman occupying roles that are normally withheld from such characters (leader, fighter, viewpoint character), but she views Claremont's transformation of the character from unremarkable to remarkable as an important cultural epoch in superhero comics.

This perspective is recapitulated by andré m. carrington in his analysis of Storm. He sees her as a character capable of undermining the fixed idea of black womanhood in favor of a rogue individualism that defies stereotype (he uses the term *negates* [91]). Arguing that "the character's multiple embodiments over time attest to the internal differentiation within each of the distinct identity formations she represents: Black, female, Black and female, superhero, Black superhero, female superhero, and Black female superhero" (96), carrington makes the point that it is Claremont's writing of the character that cultivates her complexity by revising her backstory and character, providing her with "distinguishing features as an individual" (98), and by directly exploring her relationship to her African descent. Seeing this as leading not just to the transformation of the character, but also to the transformation of the series, carrington writes:

> The issues of *X-Men* that portray Storm as a leader compose an important era in comics' history by ceding a prominent role to a Black female character. The hero and his love interest once determined the emphasis of both the mundane and genre-specific aspects of the series. Storm's leadership heralds an egalitarian future driven by interests that cross boundaries of race, nation, and gender, furthering the series' utopian message. (102)

The end result is a character who destabilizes her own original function as an ambassador for Africa amidst an international team built around mythologies of national identity. As carrington frames it, the cultivation and exploration of Storm's individualism and lived experience as a person affiliated with a wide array of cultural intersections helps the series "emerge from behind the veil of metaphor to invoke the very familiar social conditions they mediate" (116).

This perspective on Storm's intersectionality and complexity emerges very early in scholarly discourse on the character. In *Super Heroes: A Modern Mythology* (1992), one of the great early works to discuss *X-Men* comics in an academic context, Richard Reynolds provides a thorough account of Storm's station in early *X-Men* comics as a dynamic and multi-faceted character, but one who still falls into a gendered typology.

> Storm is also a focus for the opposing themes and mythologies which the X-Men embody; her character reconciles a whole gamut of conflicting myths and ideologies. An elemental force of nature, she is the least spontaneous and most withdrawn of the X-Men. Asexual (even for a superheroine) she sports perhaps the most revealing and fetishistic black costume of any 1970s Marvel or DC character. As with the Scarlet Witch, Storm's exotic sexuality is offered in the context of family and domestic life: the family being in this case the X-Men themselves. She occupies a quasi-maternal role in the dynamics of the group, distantly tolerant of the flirtatious sexuality of Nightcrawler or Wolverine. Subsequent development of the character notwithstanding, Storm's chief function in the Byrne/Claremont X-Men was to reconcile contradictions, a traditionally female role. (94)

For Reynolds, Storm remained something of a caretaker/nurturer defined largely by her gender—a role not dissimilar to Jean Grey's in Silver Age (1956–1970) *X-Men* stories (that of nurse and bearer of the desirous gazes of teammates), though here the nursemaid element is metaphorical rather than literal.

One intriguing attribute that Storm did have from the outset, however, was a connection to Wicca (Howe 197). Wicca is a badly misunderstood nature-based religion that is often shrouded in secrecy and obscured by popular myths about witchcraft. Storm is seen to worship an unspecified goddess (which is somewhat confusing given that Storm was herself worshipped as a goddess by her people in Kenya), but she does refer to the deity as "the Bright Lady," a name associated with the Wiccan goddess Luna/the Moon, as well as other primordial goddesses such as

Oshtur and the Greek goddess Gaea. Claremont would feature characters praying to the Bright Lady in his *Black Dragon* series as well, so it is not surprising that he participated in Wicca conferences and gatherings in the early 1980s, including correspondence with organizers of the 1981 Goddess Rising conference, where the organizers acknowledged enthusiasm over Storm as a character (Claremont Papers S2.II.3). What is, perhaps, surprising is that Claremont's first wife, Bonnie Wilford, was identified as a Wiccan high priestess by Claremont's collaborator John Byrne, who in response to a forum post on his website, Byrne Robotics, noted, "I don't know how much [Claremont] played into the Wicca nonsense." However, aspects of Wicca can be seen in many of Claremont's female characters, including Storm, Jean/Phoenix, Spiral (originally created by Ann Nocenti), Magik, Margali, Amanda Sefton, Selene, and the Goblin Queen.

Claremont also built a delicate, but hard to trace, thread by which we can perceive Storm as a sorceress as well as a mutant. In *Chutes and Ladders!* (*UXM* no. 160) the X-Men travel to Limbo and meet an alternate timeline version of Storm who references "the other half of my heritage: sorcery" (n.p.). She tells them that the sorcerer-villain character Belasco allowed her to study the black arts, assuming they would corrupt her. They did not. Study and heritage, of course, are not the same thing, but astute readers learn in *To the Ends of the Earth* (*New Mutants* no. 32) that Storm is a descendant of a character named Ashake, an ancient sorceress with silver hair and blue eyes who appears in yet another Claremont-authored title, *Marada the She Wolf* (from Marvel's *Epic* line). We might also note a running theme throughout *UXM* in which Storm is particularly attractive to male sorcerer figures, including Loki, Dr. Doom, and Dracula, to name just a few.

Storm's connection to sorcery in general, and Wicca in particular, links the character to a rich tradition of intersectional feminine empowerment outside of traditional gender roles. As Lynda Warwick notes,

> Feminist Wicca provides models of ways in which women can develop qualities traditionally denied women, provides teaching and role models within the Wiccan community for women to learn skills, and offers support and affirmations for lesbian as well as heterosexual women within a creative, woman-centered community. (121)

All of this is simply to say that Storm's subtle connections to Wicca may represent an important intersection of faith, race, and gender, as well as a source of inspiration for some of her nonnormative behaviors. Beyond that, these same behaviors take on greater significance to the gender performance of other characters (male and female) given Storm's position within the team as a leader, nurturer, and role model.

Indeed, for Fawaz, it is through community that Storm achieves her agency within the pages of *X-Men* comics.

> Exploring the agency afforded by her newfound kinship networks, Storm at times takes on the role of team matriarch and female confidant to her sister mutants while alternately asserting leadership of the team, a warrior protecting her fellow X-Men. Storm's feminist sensibility, then, did not emerge as a wholesale abandonment of all gendered relations but from her demand to be a free agent who chooses her own affiliations rather than allowing them to be dictated by social expectations. (150)

In this sense, Storm's identity (including her gender identity) is constructed as a complex negotiation through dialogue with various different social categories. As noted by the scholars mentioned above, these categories intersect with Storm's performance of gender in compelling and complicated ways, each meriting consideration in their own light.

Beginning with race, then, it is perhaps to Claremont's credit that a big part of Storm's process of self-definition involves reconnecting with her heritage through both sides of her family: that of her father (a photojournalist from Harlem) and that of her mother (a Kenyan tribal princess). Referring to both of these storylines, carrington views them as important pieces of Storm's transformation from a renovation of problematic stereotypes of black womanhood to a subversive and destabilizing character (92). This character arc of exploring her individual heritage is initiated early in the run, beginning in *Cry for the Children!* (*UXM* no. 122) with Storm visiting the apartment in Harlem that her family lived in. She is distressed to find her old neighborhood in a state of shocking impoverishment, and her childhood apartment occupied by violent, drug-addicted squatters who attack her. Storm is rescued by Luke Cage and Misty Knight, who then speak to her about the institutionalized prejudice of the 1970s.

Later in the run, Claremont has Ororo leave the X-Men to take a year-long pilgrimage to her own motherland. The result is *Lifedeath: From the Heart of Darkness* (*UXM* no. 198), a story with mixed results. On the one hand, exploring the concept of diaspora through Storm and its impact on her sense of self can be seen as a progressive take for a 1980s Marvel comic book. We might even apply Michelle Bumatay's perspective on how "postcolonial comics can reconstitute conventional 'image-functions' in established social texts and political systems, and present competing narratives of resistance and rights" (29). But doing so would require a very charitable reading of the story; the black characters other than Storm fail to escape from certain key stereotypes that remain in play (primitive mysticism being the most prominent).

Similarly, we could read the story's focus on diaspora as analogous to Ryan Coogler's take on Killmonger in the recent *Black Panther* film, but whereas Coogler infused his cinematic canvas with Afro-Futurist themes to create a progressive portrayal, Claremont's portrayal of Kenya fell back on certain stereotypes about the country—or even continent. As noted by Osvaldo Oyola on the comics criticism website The Middle Spaces,

> While "Lifedeath II" is a narrative departure from the rigmarole of X-Men continuity—taking a breath to try to examine the disjuncture between Ororo's African origins and her superhero identity—it still reinforces a narrative of Africa as impoverished and superstitious.... This is something that "Lifedeath II" continues to reinforce to varying degrees in service of giving Storm a depth not afforded most (if not all) black superheroes. (n.p.)

As Oyola points out, there are strong attempts at progressive representation of Storm as a black superhero, but they just don't quite pay off to the extent that a modern reader (or Claremont himself) might have hoped.

After returning from her pilgrimage, Storm challenges Cyclops (a white man) for leadership of the X-Men, wins, and becomes even more confident and self-assured. The fact that understanding her ancestral heritage helped, to some degree, to get her there is an important acknowledgment of the black experience in America. Depicting a black woman seizing power from a white man is a statement in itself, and Claremont consistently adopts strategies of validation to sell this decision to an audience unaccustomed to a black woman being placed in this position of power in superhero comics. One such strategy was to have highly masculinized white characters validate Storm's authority by deferring to her when challenged. We see this immediately in *Mind Out of Time* (*UXM* no. 142), the second part of the now-famous *Days of Future Past* storyline. In her first mission as leader of the X-Men, Storm directly challenges the white, hypermasculine, and highly insubordinate Wolverine.

The setup to this sequence has the shapeshifting Mystique impersonating Nightcrawler, leaving two Nightcrawlers on the battlefield without a clear indication of which one is real. Storm thus demands that Wolverine sheathe his claws to avoid potentially injuring the real Nightcrawler.

Wolverine rejects the order, saying, "Not a chance. We're in the middle of a fight, Storm." She then challenges him: "Sheathe them—or use them on me." Wolverine doubles down on the conflict, pointing his claws directly at Storm and declaring, "That can be arranged, babe!" But Storm does not back down, despite recognizing (in a thought bubble), "Goddess, he means it!" Nonetheless, she stands her ground. "I am leader of the X-Men. While that is so, you will use your claws when I command. No other time." Incensed, Wolverine replies, "I wouldn't take that from Cyclops!"—an accurate account based on the established dynamic between Wolverine and Cyclops, the previous X-Men leader. Again, Storm stands her ground: "You will take it from me. You possess speed, strength—your unbreak-able adamantium skeleton makes you nearly invulnerable. You should not need your claws except in the most extreme of situations against the deadliest and most powerful of foes." And with that, Wolverine relents, sheathing his claws (17).

Although it is difficult not to read Storm's sheathing of Wolverine's claws as a symbolic emasculation, such an interpretation might undermine some of the strong gender work that Claremont was already doing with the Logan/Wolverine character in relationship to Logan's complex nego-tiation of masculinity (a subject I take up in chapter 5). The greater point is that Storm's leadership role, one that broke through long-held racial and gender barriers in superhero comics, is directly validated through a strong and victorious opposition to an iconic, hypermasculine white character. Storm's ability to succeed through empathy and compassion—explaining her decision rather than simply butting heads, as Cyclops used to—is like-wise telling of her character.

Later in the run, Claremont would use Cyclops again to further validate Storm's role as leader of the X-Men. Indeed, the Storm/Cyclops relationship is pivotal for advancing Storm to the forefront of the run, a role she never really relinquished. Cyclops's validation of Storm's leader-ship abilities pushes the reader to accept a major status shift. The relation-ship is based on mutual respect, competition, and a shared understanding of the unique burden of leading the X-Men.

Cyclops is the lone holdover from the original X-Men team created in the 1960s by Jack Kirby and Stan Lee, who portrayed him as a gifted leader who had earned his position. In the 1970s, as Marvel was moving to an international team (aiming to increase sales with an international market [Howe 154]), Cyclops was a white, heterosexual male Ameri-can, a familiar character who establishes continuity with the previous series. In early issues of the new series he remained the leader and was featured prominently on covers. As our research shows, he also had the most narrative captions, making him the main viewpoint character before Storm took that role from him as well—another exchange of power between Storm and Cyclops, whose relationship is deeply pivotal to defining her authority.

In *Reunion* (*UXM* no. 154), Claremont portrays a scene of mutual admiration and competition between Storm and Cyclops as they play a superhero version of handball. Storm is the leader at this point, but Cyclops's return presents a threat. The dialogue in the scene reads as follows:

> **Storm:** Your point. We're tied once more. That was a very nice—and nasty—move, Scott. Wolverine would have been proud of you.
> **Cyclops:** Consider it my swansong. I'm beat.
> **Storm:** I, too, shall we call this a draw?
> **Cyclops:** The latest in a series. The games I win with experience are balanced by the ones you win with skill and vice versa. You're very good.
> **Storm:** You sound surprised.
> **Cyclops:** I like being the best. It's not easy getting used to having a rival, much less an equal. (n.p.)

Immediately thereafter, the conclusions reached in handball are verified in the real world, with Cyclops and Storm narrowly escaping an alien attack in which she demonstrates her power and capability, solidifying for the reader that her claim to leadership is valid, and she is more than just a fill-in for Cyclops.

This competition is taken to a logical extreme in *Duel* (*UXM* no. 201) when, as mentioned above, Storm (who has lost the ability to use her superpowers) defeats Cyclops in single combat for leadership of the X-Men. In this issue, the torch is most clearly and most inarguably passed, leaving Claremont's team, at last, fully detached from the Silver Age. In later years, and on different teams, Storm and Cyclops would continue to challenge each other, question each other's choices, and generally hold each other accountable—to their benefit and that of their respective teams.

Storm's progression from stereotypical character to progressive representation is reflected in a comparative analysis of her portrayal in the first twelve issues of the Claremont run and the overall run (fig. 2.2). Most notably, the increase in the number of Storm's thought bubbles, giving readers growing exposure to her interior monologue as a viewpoint character, is enormous—more than double, in fact—and her speech bubbles (reflecting her voice within the narrative world) increase dramatically at the same time.

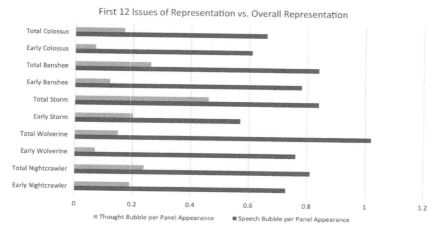

**Fig. 2.2.** *Variation in short-term versus long-term character representation.*

As Storm develops agency as a leader and prominent character, the portrayal of her sexuality begins to move in new directions as well, slowly transitioning the character from dehumanized sex object (very much in keeping with gender norms in Marvel comics of the time) to a woman with sexual agency and desire within the narrative world of *X-Men* comics. Interestingly, some of this humanization work is initially created by surfacing and deconstructing the damsel-in-distress role that is so familiar to comics readers. As Cooper notes,

> So, when challenged to take Storm through a parallel trajectory [to that of Phoenix] (exploring the ways in which women sometimes sublimate sexuality to achieve power, sublimate power to achieve sexuality or integrate both into something genuinely transcendent), [Claremont] started writing stories in which Storm and those around her—from Professor X to Dr. Doom, from Dracula to the denizens of Asgard—become hyperaware of her sex appeal only to realize how secondary it is to her other virtues. (195)

Cooper frames these stories as a sort of response to Jean Grey's turn as Phoenix and then Dark Phoenix. In Cooper's eyes, Storm's character is largely developed around this tragic parallel to Jean Grey, whose corruption and passing is framed as a sort of canary in a coal mine to Ororo's frequently teased potential destruction at the hands of her own Phoenixlike powers.

Margaret Galvan offers a similar perspective but sees the relationship as progressive, with Jean's death marking the long-term failure of liberal feminism in the 1970s, and Storm's survival marking the success of that same project in the 1980s (49). This parallel reading and its divergent results present Ororo as an alternative to Jean, a success story in contrast to Jean's failure, thus leveraging the long-standing gravitas of the *Dark Phoenix Saga* into a testament of Ororo's strength as a character—something that Dr. Doom and Loki seem to recognize before the majority of *UXM* readers came around to the concept. Nonetheless, again we find Storm's agency validated by the expressed opinion and admiration of powerful white male characters.

Claremont would next give Storm a more literal gender-queerness, while simultaneously cultivating her character's sexual agency. As noted above by Reynolds, Storm's early portrayals can fit nicely into the paradigm of virginal sexuality that Marvel comics of the era had adopted pretty widely by focusing on beautiful, sexualized female characters who had no sense of their own sexuality, let alone a desire to explore it.

Initially, Storm's lack of sexual desire is framed largely through her decision to characterize her relationship to her teammates as more of a sibling connection than a romantic one. As a result of this choice by the character (and Claremont), "[i]n a series that often revolves around the romantic pairing of characters, she is not one of the cogs in the relationship wheel" (Darowski, *X-Men* 68). But while the romantic lives of all the other *X-Men* characters are explored through relationship story arcs, Storm does not get such a portrayal until a pair of relationships later in the run. This absence of sexual desire and sexual agency is perhaps problematic in light of gender roles in Marvel comics of the time. Scott Bukatman observes that "Female desire is absent—when male creators design women characters, they continue to indulge male fantasies" (66). This is simply to say that the norm in comics of the time was to portray female characters who are sexy to the reader, but who have no sexual desires of their own.

This changes for Storm when she finally has a romantic story arc with Yukio (subtextually) and then Forge (canonically). This is the main thesis of my chapter in *Supersex*, "Storm of Passion," in which I argue that "the key to Storm's symbolic capital is her transition from a passive sexual fantasy object to a dynamic character with sexual agency" (79), a transition that is spurred specifically by exploring her relationships to other characters.

The first seeds of Storm's transition toward a presentation of direct gender-queerness are planted in an encounter with a group of subterranean mutant refugees, called the Morlocks, living in the tunnels of the New York City sewer system. Claremont uses the Morlocks to create a mutant class hierarchy, allowing *UXM* to speak to issues of class, privilege, and visibility in a way that the traditional superhero narrative (with its casual portrayal of wealth) often avoids. Their name is, of course, a reference to H. G. Wells's *The Time Machine*, in which the Morlocks are tunnel-dwelling cannibals from a future society where class differences had led to evolutionary differences, eventually making the upper and lower classes completely distinct species. In *UXM* the Morlocks serve as the mutant underclass, with most of the narrative tension (voiced by their leader, the highly androgynous Callisto) manifesting around bitterness and hatred toward the privileged mutant class, the X-Men, who live in a mansion and have a jet.

This portrayal has the potential to reaffirm class distinctions by demonizing the lower class, except Callisto is portrayed as noble and heroic, and her speeches become increasingly sensible as the Claremont run progresses. The Morlocks also offer important intersectional commentary on the concept of passing, thus creating some interesting subjects for an intersectional approach to feminism once again. These metaphors get hammered home dramatically during the events of the *Mutant Massacre* storyline (*UXM* nos. 210–213), in which the Morlocks are the frontline victims of (what appears to be) an anti-mutant hate crime.

In her first encounter with Callisto, Storm is forced to depart from normative gender roles by getting her hands dirty, asserting her position as leader of the X-Men (again, abnormal for a female character at the time) and dueling Callisto (seemingly to the death) in a knife fight to decide leadership of the Morlocks. Storm wins and now finds herself the leader of both the X-Men and the Morlocks. As a personification of class discrepancy and gender nonconformity, Callisto surfaces key social categories in Storm's character through contrast. And while Storm's defeat of Callisto might initially read as a sort of symbolic homogenization, their relationship will become increasingly complex over the years, with Callisto serving as both inspiration and mentor to Storm in a literal sense, but also metaphorically as an important symbol of the nonconformity that Storm aspires to.

Interestingly, Callisto would later become the focus of one of the better interrogations of gender-queerness. She is one of the most obviously gender-queer characters in the entirety of Claremont's run, to such a degree that later authors (and even Wikipedia) failed to grasp his complex treatment of the character's relationship to her gender in a notable story. For context, in Greek mythology, Callisto was a follower of Artemis, goddess of the hunt. After Zeus falls in love with Callisto, he transforms into Artemis to trick her into sleeping with him. In *UXM* nos. 259–263, Claremont's Callisto is captured by a rival Morlock, Masque, who alters her appearance to make her look like a supermodel, a highly feminized symbol. The X-Man Colossus becomes obsessed with her and sees beyond the illusion (through a combination of his supressed memories and his artist's soul). According to *Wikipedia* ("Callisto [comics]") and a later *UXM* writer, Scott Lobdell (*UXM* nos. 291–293), Masque tortured Callisto by taking away her newly gifted beauty, which would make Callisto align with gender-normalizing fairy-tale princesses to some degree. However, a close reading of Claremont's scenes shows the opposite. For Callisto, the supermodel aesthetic is the cruelty. She describes it as "a mask that defines my life and being that I can't ever be rid of." She feels commodified by it, telling Peter, "All I am anymore, Peter, is a package" (*The Lower Depths* [*UXM* no. 253] 18).

In Claremont's hands, Callisto's story is one of gender deviance that expresses the damaging effects of literal forced gender performance in contrast to the freedom and power that Callisto had once achieved (and continued to desire) by rejecting the norm. In her later incarnation, she is just another archetypal witch character filled with rage over her lost beauty, a take that ultimately validates existing gender roles. The fact that a later writer and an errant modern-day Wikipedia contributor both completely failed to see the underlying message of Callisto's story is testament to Claremont's progressiveness and to the queerness of Callisto as a character. In hindsight, Callisto's first encounter with Storm seems to have spurred Storm's transition to a gender-queer presentation in the issues that would follow.

Immediately after Storm's duel with Callisto, the X-Men travel to Japan, where Storm has a random encounter with a woman named Yukio. Interestingly, Yukio destabilizes the gender performance of at least two *X-Men* characters within the Claremont run. For Wolverine, she contradicts his aspirations to pursue romances with effeminate (or hyper-effeminate) women such as Jean Grey and Mariko Yashida, thus complicating the otherwise simplistic Beauty and the Beast paradigm that Wolverine can sometimes fall into (something I discuss in chapter 5). To Storm, however, Yukio offers a way of living outside the feminine stereotype of the goddess that Ororo, by virtue of her powers, has fallen into. Yukio's impact on Ororo is immediately transformative (including her costume) (fig. 2.3). The fact that Storm's transformation is spurred by her relationship with Yukio (and comes just a few issues after her first encounter with

**Fig. 2.3.** *Storm debuts her new costume in* To Have and Have Not *(UXM, vol. 1, no. 173).*
*Paul Smith, penciler.*

Callisto) is again telling of her intersectional identity. As established in my
essay "Storm of Passion" (Deman 83–87), Storm's relationship with Yukio
is subtextually sexual, and we see Storm's sexuality defining her resistance
to stereotype quite directly.

Storm doesn't just escape the goddess role here, however, but also the
(potentially overlapping) nurturer role, as revealed through Kitty Pryde's
appalled reaction to Storm's transformation. Prior to this scene, Storm had
formed a quasi-maternal relationship with Kitty. Carol Cooper says that
because their relationship is one "deprived of romantic distractions and
similar forms of emotional intimacy, [Storm's] bond with Kitty became
particularly close, almost that of a child and surrogate mother" (191).
Of all the characters impacted by Storm's transformation from goddess
to punk, Kitty took it the hardest, perceiving it as a betrayal. However,
carrington sees this as a symbolically important disentanglement of Storm
from a black caregiver stereotype.

> In the spectacle of Storm's transformation, her relationship to
> young Kitty Pryde models the ways in which White Americans have
> learned to perceive women of African descent as caretakers. Despite
> the many routes they have taken in matters of work and family, Black
> women have been associated with mothering other people's chil-
> dren, particularly White children, since the era of slavery. (97)

The suggestion is that Kitty has transferred a symbolic archetype onto Storm, even if unconsciously. In Cooper's view, "One of the most interesting things Claremont did with young Kitty Pryde was show that even the most progressive postmodern female can still hold other women to unrealistic standards of stereotypical or conformist behaviour" (191). Like all stereotypes, it is one that limits Storm's ability to operate as an individual with agency rather than as someone who simply internalizes the roles that others expect her to fill. Kitty is a lonely kid away from her family for the first time, in desperate need of mothering, but perhaps she slots Ororo/Storm into that role too readily, thus unfairly placing an enormous responsibility on her within the context of carrington's argument. This perceived betrayal can then be integrated into the other emancipatory elements of Storm's transformation.

We can complicate the matter even further by reading Storm's capacity for speaking to class division as part of this same transformation. Over the course of the *UXM* series, Storm is both a goddess and an orphan, a consort to kings and a switchblade-wielding punk, a privileged mansion dweller and a common thief. She has experienced life at both ends of the social ladder. As we see in this chapter, scholars have paid a great deal of attention to Storm's race and gender—particularly with regard to her capacity to destabilize both—but another representational attribute worth discussing is this perspective on the extremes of class division: rich and poor.

Storm's initial costume design speaks to this, featuring symbols of regal wealth, including a flowing cape, gold coloring, a large jewel, and a tiara. After her transformation, however, she rejects this costume in favor of the punk look seen in figure 2.3. As articulated by Neil Eriksen, punk rock was "a working class sub-cultural response to the conditions of existence of sections of the working and unemployed youth centered around the musical expression of punk rock" ("Pop Culture" n.p.). Storm's transition to a punk style—which occurs in response to a pair of similarly punk characters (Callisto and Yukio)—can thus be read (in part) as an indictment of the class privilege that she had felt was containing and limiting her individual expression once again. Speaking more broadly, Storm's negotiation of class divides is a steady thread for her character, surfacing prominently in her aforementioned visit to Harlem (*Cry for the Children!*), her pilgrimage to Kenya (*Lifedeath: From the Heart of Darkness*), her partnership with the thief Gambit (*Gambit: Out of the Frying Pan*), and many other stories. Thus, class—like sexuality, religion, and race—adds an important emancipatory element to the character's performance of gender.

Indeed, all of these intersections contribute to the rich tapestry of a complex character who defies prescriptive gender roles in comics just by existing in the way that she does, and then more so by continuing to push against the standards of the comics medium through a series of complex, intersecting social categories, all to such an extent that this one chapter can barely scratch the surface of Storm's significance.

Perhaps the best way to close this chapter, then, is with a testament to the intensity of Claremont's relationship to Storm, a character he created. As our data clearly indicates, he loved her, but we can extrapolate a similar conclusion through qualitative means as well. Storm is the subject of a notable Claremont story that features an author-surrogate finding inspiration to carry on with his writing thanks to an encounter with her. *Hope* (*Classic X-Men* no. 11) features a backup story by Claremont in which a British author (Claremont himself was London born) faces an existential crisis after working as a writer for a nondescript fantasy publisher (an obvious stand-in for Marvel Comics). The character, Phil, also specifically mentions his admiration for *Eagle* comics anthologies and *Dan Dare*, both of which Claremont mentioned in an interview when asked how he first discovered comics (DeFalco 58). Thus, the author-surrogate function is readily implied.

Through Phil, Claremont seems to give voice to his own doubts about his career choices. Reflecting on his legacy as a pop culture writer, Phil laments,

> Years, I've spent at your grindstone, Reg—honing my craft, building my rep—I broke my back for the company. Why can't you be satisfied with that?! An' it's never the second-rate work that gets grief, invariably the top-notch stories. The stuff I put my heart into. I'm proudest of. I care the most about. . . . How often have you been told, 'nobody forces you to work here, Phil.' So why don't I leave? No guts. I'll always be more scared of what I'm giving up than what I might gain. Too bloody comfortable. (n.p.)

Phil then wanders into an abandoned office tower and walks to the edge of the roof, wanting "so much and nothing more so than oblivion," at which point Storm flies down and tells him, "You should not stand so near the edge" (n.p.), a declaration that lends itself to figurative as well as literal interpretation. Guessing Phil's suicidal intent, Storm takes him flying on a gust of wind to help him experience the joy he has forgotten. The story ends with Storm declaring, "While you live, you hope. And with hope, there are always possibilities," to which Phil replies, "Maybe and maybe not. The choice is mine" (n.p.).

Interpreting Phil as an author-surrogate offers potential insight into Storm's importance for Claremont and the extent to which his engagement with that character helped to sustain and drive *UXM* narratives to the heights of symbolic capital that they achieved. Storm was neither Claremont's first nor last subject through which to interrogate and complicate gender roles in comics, but she might be his largest and most expansive, a complicated woman existing at the nexus of numerous identity markers.

# CHAPTER 3

# *Ladies Night* and the Second Generation of Claremont Women

> I wanted to establish her absolutely as "this was the Betsy I had in mind, back when we started." The idea of her being . . . she's the one who always wanted to be the superhero. The hero. Brian was the bookish, pipe-smoking one.
>
> –CHRIS CLAREMONT, FROM A WOMEN WRITE ABOUT COMICS INTERVIEW

While Claremont's ambitions regarding intersectional feminism can best be seen in his articulation of Storm, he also populated his world with a broader cosmology of women characters that could contribute to the overall commentary on gender roles in the series by adding numerous different perspectives. Importantly, these additional *X-Men* characters created a spectrum of gender roles, gender performance, gender conformity, and gender deviancy.

The first of these new X-Women was Kitty Pryde, a thirteen-year-old girl (and Marvel's first canonically Jewish superhero) who joins the X-Men in the immediate aftermath of the *Dark Phoenix Saga*, effectively assuming Jean Grey's spot on the team. As with Sam Langsdale's reading of Phoenix (discussed in chapter 1), scholars have often associated Kitty with the philosophical perspectives of Donna Harraway. In her essay "From Kitty to Cat: Kitty Pryde and the Phases of Feminism," Margaret Galvan argues that the character can be seen as representing transgressive gender politics in a manner that brings to mind Harraway's conception of cyborg feminism. This theory is notoriously complex, but, in general, it is the notion that being seen as abnormal (transgressive) can be empowering because it removes the pressure to conform, thus freeing the subject. For Galvan, Kitty is one of the rare comic book characters from the 1980s who can embody these symbols. Kitty's ability to "phase" through solid matter challenges "notions of stability at their most basic, physical level. How she employs these transgressive powers in concert with a plucky persona make Pryde an often-overlooked powerhouse and a figure of the multivalent feminism that thrived in the 1980s" (47–48).

Kitty is a teenage mutant Jewish girl genius, and all of these aspects define her, even (if not especially) when they intersect and create friction. The result, according to Galvan, is that "All of these simultaneously ever-present identities embody the concerns of 1980s feminism by putting pressure on monolithic ideas of identity" (50). She also notes that Kitty's transgressive potential manifests multiple times throughout the Claremont run, with Kitty frequently criticizing other characters for thinking within a one-dimensional paradigm. Kitty thus vocalizes the same transgressive attributes that she embodies. As Galvan concludes, "She acts as a complex, multifaceted character who does not simply regurgitate feminist politics, but who actively engages in feminist practice and continually subverts patriarchal expectations with her transgressive body" (56–57).

The next X-Woman to join the team was Rogue. Like Kitty, she is a teenager, but Rogue is also someone who first came into the book as a villain after being radicalized as a youth by her foster parents, the villains Mystique and Destiny. Also, whereas Kitty occupied the traditionally masculine role of viewpoint character in the sidekick tradition, Rogue would occupy the position of bruiser thanks to a combination of super strength and an aggressive villain-appropriate attitude. Her relationship to gender performance is, like Storm's, intersectional in nature. As Anthony Michael D'Agostino notes in his reading of the character,

> Rogue's relationship to difference so representative of the figure of the superhero's anti-identitarian queerness, I argue, is largely a result of Claremont's attempts to embody the agonism of feminist identity politics, thus suggesting that Claremont's superhero comics constitute their own queer feminism. (259)

As with Galvan's reading of Kitty, D'Agostino sees Rogue as an intersectional figure who adds yet another transgressive female character to the *X-Men* roster.

Claremont next introduced Rachel Summers, a time-displaced *X-Men* character suffering from PTSD and simmering rage. Rachel would challenge gender roles through androgynous clothes and through her experience of intense suffering within the pages of *UXM*, a role traditionally afforded to masculine protagonists in the Dostoyevsky vein. Claremont's portrayal of Rachel is perhaps his most tragic of any *X-Men* character. She fails to integrate into the found family of the X-Men and is unable to control her anger, leading to a standoff in which Wolverine stabs her to prevent her from taking a life. From there, Rachel leaves the book, only to return months later in the *X-Men* spinoff *Excalibur*.

Each of these Claremont Women deserves to be studied at length, but in the interest of the economy of the broader argument that I wish to make in this book, I have decided to focus instead on a pair of X-Women who have not been studied to nearly the extent that the above-mentioned female characters have been, Elizabeth Braddock (Betsy)/Psylocke and Alison Blaire/Dazzler.

In the back half of the Claremont run (beginning in the mid-1980s), one of the more nuanced commentaries on gender roles comes through the character of Elizabeth Braddock, aka Psylocke. Like other characters who were either cultivated or created by Claremont, Psylocke would become a prominent female sex symbol in comics after she "was turned into the murderous Lady Mandarin, a fetishized Asian sex object in the style of the classic Dragon Lady of the 1930s" (Lam n.p.). This would develop after Psylocke's infamous "race swap," from Caucasian to Asian, a storyline that has frequently been called out for its insensitive treatment of East Asian culture. Rather than ignore this metaphorical elephant in the room, I thought it best to speak to this issue first because it is one that dominates discussions of Psylocke, often overshadowing the ways in which the character performs femininity.

During the *Acts of Vengeance* storyline (1989), the white X-Man Psylocke is physically transfigured into an Asian woman by a villain seeking to brainwash her and turn her into an elite assassin for a group of ninja warriors in the Marvel Universe. In an interview with Claire Napier, Claremont described the transformation as a simple disguise element to allow Psylocke to rule the Hong Kong underworld; it was intended to be temporary but was made permanent in response to fan reaction. Just as giving blue eyes to the most prominent African American comics character (an important complication of Storm's racial embodiment that predates Claremont's tenure on the series) met with criticism, giving a British consciousness and heritage to what was instantly the most prominent Asian superhero in Marvel comics was, justifiably, met with criticism.

As mentioned, that criticism has, historically, overshadowed Betsy/Psylocke's commentary on gender performance prior to her body swap. In 1976 Claremont created the character for the eighth issue of *Captain Britain*, titled *Riot on Regent Street*. She was the sister of the eponymous hero, Brian Braddock, and in keeping with Claremont's fixation on female pilots (again, his mother was a pilot and worked for the RAF), Betsy was a charter pilot. After Claremont left the book in 1982, Alan Moore inherited the character, establishing her now-iconic purple hair color before the character was passed on to writers Jamie Delano and then Alan Davis. In one notable story from *Captain Britain*, in an issue titled *It's Hard to Be a*

*Hero*, written and drawn by Alan Davis, Betsy briefly takes on the mantle of Captain Britain herself, only to be brutally beaten and have her eyes gouged out by the villain Slaymaster. This story was Davis's first writing credit on *Captain Britain* (a title he had been illustrating for some time). Davis would go on to become a talented and accomplished writer/artist, but this issue features a textbook example of fridging: Betsy takes on a traditionally masculine role and is immediately humiliated and put in her place. Her maiming is used at the narrative level to incentivize her brother, and the brutal violence that Betsy is subjected to ultimately leads to her loss of power when it reverts to her brother, forcing her into retirement.

Claremont reclaimed and rehabilitated Psylocke less than a year after her blinding. In the issue *Why Do We Do These Things We Do?* (illustrated by Alan Davis), Psylocke is given back her sight and her sense of purpose, and even allowed to outshine her brother (who also appears in the issue) before finding her place in the X-Universe. Her redemption and reintegration into a heroic community is, in many ways, quite similar to the character recovery work that Claremont famously performed on Carol Danvers/Ms. Marvel just a few years prior. In that case he "use[d] the character's own voice to push back against a story he (and others) felt did an injustice to a character he cared about, and pull[ed] that character in his orbit to continue writing her" (Cocca 193).[1] We can see something very similar happening in Claremont's reclamation of Psylocke.

Once he brought Betsy/Psylocke into the world of *X-Men*, Claremont quickly established her as a 100 percent valid and legitimate hero. If anything, she has an excess of the heroic spirit, a depiction that allows the character to move beyond a rough turn in the character's history to become an elite Marvel superhero. The recovery of the character from the trope of fridging is itself a form of gender deviancy, but from there Claremont continued to unsettle gender roles through Psylocke by surfacing the tension between her visual appearance and internal desires.

Visually, Psylocke appears to be a hyperbolic projection of effeminate characteristics to the point of collapse. At the beginning of her X-Men career, Psylocke (still in her original body) is presented with a highly effeminate pink costume (fig. 3.1), but when not in costume, she dresses more like a 1950s governess than a modern woman. Her hair is immaculately coiffed, and she smiles congenially. Speaking once again to intersectionality, Psylocke's performance of femininity is entangled in her relation to economic and social class. She is the child of successful, wealthy parents and holds a reputable name in international society. As such, her adherence to outdated modes of femininity can be seen as an assertion of class

**Fig. 3.1.** *Psylocke's first costume as seen in* Psylocke *(UXM, vol. 1, no. 213). Alan Davis, penciler.*

identity and obligation. Behind her proper presentation, however, her thoughts and actions run contrary to the hyperfeminine, class-defined role that she performs.

Our data supports this observation in some intriguing ways. The average number of scenes showing an X-Woman visibly crying is 6.18; the average number of scenes with an X-Man crying is 1.42. Psylocke, however, sheds an on-panel tear only once, and as part of a hallucination. (The character crying is not really her, but a phantasm of herself that she encounters.) When the character is depicted in real-world settings of the Claremont run, she does not cry. In contrast, Dazzler, who joins the team at about the same time as Psylocke, is seen crying on three separate occasions in that same approximate span, and Rogue (who joined years before Psylocke) is seen crying nine times after Psylocke joins the X-Men. The male characters Havok and Longshot are each shown in tears twice during that same time period. But instead of crying, Betsy/Psylocke's reaction to frightening situations is often to smile, and her response to sorrowful occurrences is to get angry. Even Wolverine can be seen crying more often than Psylocke does. If we interpret crying as a symbol of emotional eruption, or vulnerability, or even a stereotype of femininity, Psylocke does not conform to these potentially gendered expectations.

Another way that Psylocke challenges the soap opera stereotype of women being primarily interested in relationships is that she has no romantic relationships in *UXM* (though a brief flirtation with the underage Doug Ramsay—coinciding with her first X-Universe appearance, in *Why Do We Do These Things We Do?*—lingers to some degree). Despite all her years on the series, Psylocke has only one on-panel kiss, and its context is very telling of her nature, as will be discussed below. She is also one of only four *X-Men* characters who average more than one speech bubble per panel appearance. Despite being a junior character for much of the Claremont run, she makes her voice heard quite frequently.

Moving into qualitative analysis, Psylocke is perceived from the outset as capable thanks to an earlier character-defining battle with a hypermasculine villain character—Sabretooth—in the story *Psylocke* from *UXM* no. 213. Sabretooth had been established one issue prior as a reflective foil to Logan/Wolverine who embraces and projects the same masculine tropes of primal masculinity that define Logan (tropes that will be taken up in chapter 5). Despite being badly outmatched (Sabretooth is an accomplished killer, largely immune to Psylocke's telepathy), Psylocke singlehandedly holds him off in a physical confrontation despite having no physical superpowers, thus earning the respect of her peers and admission to the team as an X-Man. This display of dominance by a powerless heroine who defeats a superpowered alpha male is deeply reminiscent of Storm's defeat of Cyclops for leadership of the X-Men (discussed in chapter 2).

Wolverine himself provides the assessment and interprets the meaning of Psylocke's victory over Sabretooth:

> When the crunch came, she didn't fold. She thought of the X-Men before herself—even though we'd all put her down pretty hard. Handled herself real well, too. Ask me, she's proved herself—an' then some. If it's what she wants she's an X-Man. (23)

Psylocke affirms that being an X-Man is indeed what she wants, and Storm (team leader at the time) notes that Wolverine speaks for them all in his assessment before officially welcoming her to the team.

Shortly thereafter, Claremont escalates Psylocke's gender-deviant portrayal by granting her a pragmatic callousness that stands in sharp contrast to the soft gentility expressed by her outward appearance, again creating a compelling juxtaposition between outward appearance and inward constitution that suggests the artificiality of Psylocke's hyperfeminine exterior. In *UXM* no. 219, Psylocke suggests an extreme response when former X-Man Havok eavesdrops on a team strategy meeting during the *Mutant Massacre* storyline: "He heard our discussion, Storm, he knows too much. I dare not attempt another mindwipe, but, as well, we dare not leave him loose where the Marauders can get at him [and torture him for information]." In response, Storm asks, "We have any other option?" Psylocke replies, "Wolverine's. Kill him." Havok notes in an internal monologue that Psylocke is 100 percent serious in this suggestion. Storm, after considering it, says, "No, Psylocke. We do not slay our own" (*Where Duty Lies* 22–23). The juxtaposition here thrives within the multimodal nature of the comics form. Watching a woman with bouffant hair and a flowing pink dress advocate for the tactical murder of an innocent superhero can be jarring.

It is not, however, inconsistent with the violent tendencies of Psylocke's character. Speaking again to our statistical sample, she has the highest kill-count of any X-Man, male or female, with five on-panel kills (so long as we do not count Dark Phoenix, who otherwise wins by a factor of a billion by incidentally killing an entire planet in the *Dark Phoenix Saga*). All of Psylocke's kills occur in a single issue, *I Am Lady Mandarin*, after she is brainwashed by the villain Mandarin. The fact that she is not in her right mind at the time puts an asterisk beside this finding, but it is still a brutal portrayal of human slaughter enacted by an X-Man and thus still reads as divergent from the gender norms of comics at the time.

Peter Coogan famously observed that comic book superheroes' costumes represents their innate character (90). This does not work for Psylocke unless the innate character is read as somehow ironic. Psylocke's preposterously effeminate puffy pink costume and her warrior spirit might thereby be explained through the concept of "the feminine masquerade," a theory that posits the deconstructive power of over-the-top portrayals of femininity. The concept began with the work of psychologist Joan Riviere before being picked up by legendary Freud disciple Jacques Lacan to explain a woman's sometimes ironic relationship to her own understanding of gender.

In her 1929 paper "Womanliness as a Masquerade," Riviere suggests that women wanting to participate in patriarchal society will often don a mask of femininity to appear subservient to the prevailing world order and thus nonthreatening to their male counterparts (303–305). The idea is that women will wear femininity as a mask of conformity, but they may often take that disguise beyond its reasonable expectations to emphasize the artifice, to showcase that it is in fact a mask, fake and unnatural. This same masquerade can be applied to Psylocke as a way of understanding her performance of gender as deeply ironic, yet necessary if she is going to participate in the masculinized superhero culture that she desperately desires to be a part of.

This reading is perhaps most apparent in *Lost in the Funhouse* (*UXM Annual* no. 11), in which Claremont takes Psylocke's disguise off, both literally and metaphorically. The issue features a supernatural contrivance that grants each X-Man their heart's true desire. It is in this same issue that Storm's enduring love for Yukio is made clear. For Psylocke, her heart's desire is to peel off her costume (and its outward symbolism) along with her very skin (the veneer of humanity that she conforms to) to reveal a robotlike warrior underneath (fig. 3.2).

Her family runs away horrified by this reveal, escaping into their own desire: a domestic life of child-rearing and sweater-wearing. Psylocke stares after them, saying, "Am I so fearful? I suppose the warrior always is. Be happy with your heart's desire, Brian, as I shall be with mine." Storm interjects a simple "I am sorry," to which Betsy replies, "I, too, in a way, for innocence lost. I thought my past had made me hard, as deadly in my own way as Wolverine. But this is how I was born. My life merely served to temper and hone the steel that already existed" (*Lost in the Funhouse* 30). The desire that Psylocke expresses is not just to be a warrior. It is also to live honestly—to reveal herself to those she loves most, thus reflecting the burden of disguise that the feminine masquerade has placed upon her. Shortly after this reveal, Psylocke will debut a new costume featuring body armor, a mask, and a deep hood, all amounting to a significantly less feminine outward appearance.

Although not commonly discussed, Psylocke briefly becomes field leader of the X-Men after the apparent death of Storm in *The Cradle Will Fall* (*UXM* no. 248). Interestingly, she achieves this mantle undemocratically. Betsy/Psylocke simply claims the mantle of leadership unilaterally by issuing orders to Havok in the next issue. When Havok notes, "You talk like you're boss," Betsy simply asks, "[D]oes that bother you?" Havok replies, "Frankly—yes." Betsy says, "Find me someone better, I shall step aside," and continues giving the orders from there (*The Dane Curse* 15).

Psylocke's first mission as team leader is successful and is quickly followed by her last, in which her precognitive abilities (or perhaps just a telepathic connection with a precognitive mutant named Gateway) tell her that the X-Men are walking into a trap at the hands of their foes, the Reavers, one that will result in them all dying. To prevent this, she again acts unilaterally, and also without the consent of her fellow team members,

**Fig. 3.2.** *Psylocke's warrior fantasy portrayed in* Lost in the Funhouse (UXM Annual, *vol. 1, no. 11). Alan Davis, penciler.*

manipulating them into walking through the Siege Perilous (a device that scatters them across the globe, erasing all memories and furnishing them with new identities). Havok, however, resists, questioning her logic, at which point we see Psylocke's butterfly flare activate (a visual symbol that she is using her telepathic powers), clearly indicating that she is manipulating his consciousness (thus crossing a major moral boundary evident throughout Claremont's run, in which he often used telepathy to explore the concept of consent). For good measure, Psylocke kisses Havok—her only on-panel kiss in the Claremont run.

That Psylocke's only kiss would come within the context of a strategic move is telling, once again, of the character's sociopathic nature. With that kiss, she sends Alex/Havok on his way, but she hangs around just long enough to taunt her enemies before disappearing through the Siege Perilous herself. All in all, she saves the X-Men's lives, but in a very authoritarian way that again showcases a unilateral infliction of her will alongside a willingness to overstep ethical boundaries (particularly in contrast to other X-Men leaders such as Cyclops, Storm, Nightcrawler, and Wolverine). This moral fluidity is native to Psylocke's character and can, again, be read as gender deviant by the (implicitly white, heterosexual) standards of the superhero genre in the 1980s.

Although the team was dissolved at this point in *X-Men* continuity, Psylocke's story would continue. Like the device used in *Lost in the Funhouse* (*UXM Annual* no. 11), the Siege Perilous would grant those who pass through it a new life that reflects their desires, thus providing expository evidence of character motivation. The goddess Roma, who gifts the Siege Perilous to them, describes its properties as follows:

> Know, X-Men, that the Siege Perilous is for your use as well. As Avalon was for King Arthur, so may the siege be for you. A release from the trials and travails of this world. . . . Gateway to a paradise well earned . . . if such is your desire. (*Down Under* 29)

Even though the Siege will judge the X-Men, Roma assures them they will pass that test, so for them it will provide a paradise-like reward. Colossus becomes an artist, Dazzler a movie star, and Havok a soldier. The Siege delivers Psylocke directly to Marvel's most famous ninja clan, The Hand, best known from the pages of Frank Miller's run on *Daredevil*. It is here that she undergoes her race swap, but in the process she becomes a physically powerful assassin as well, granting her an outward appearance and power set that truly reflect her inner being for the first time in the character's history. In fact, her new costume is nearly identical to that of Elektra, an iconic Marvel warrior woman.

The brainwashing process by which Betsy/Psylocke is transformed is the subject of *The Key That Breaks the Locke* (*UXM* no. 256). Here Claremont depicts the internal workings of Betsy's mind as a dream-logic landscape while she undergoes her transition from psychic to psychic ninja. The issue takes the classic heel-turn story and turns it into a character-revealing psychodrama as Psylocke murders her way through visions of her character's comics continuity in order to finally achieve the power that Slaymaster's violent attack took from her when he blinded her in the pages of *Captain Britain*.

The sequence in *The Key That Breaks the Locke* opens with a portrayal of Betsy's early relationship to her brother Brian (the man who will become Captain Britain) when they were school-age children, revealing her tomboy nature, her lonely upbringing, and her desire for fantasy adventure juxtaposed with her fear of achieving that. Later, she reflects on her envy of Brian becoming Captain Britain and reveals Psylocke's fear of her own interior numbness to a dream version of Storm (echoing *Lost in the Funhouse*). She recounts her own failure as Captain Britain, cursing her weakness before attacking Ororo in rage. From there, in pursuit of power, Psylocke easily dispatches dream versions of each of her former X-Men comrades, all part of The Hand's plan to have her "execute" her heroic self in order to be reborn as their puppet. The plan is interrupted, however, when Slaymaster arrives in the dream (against The Hand's intention) to force Psylocke to face her ultimate character-defining moment: the time she attempted to be Captain Britain and was violently assaulted and brutally blinded.

Through all of this, Claremont ties together decades of Betsy/Psylocke's continuity across multiple authors and franchises to form a cohesive vision of a traumatized person who hated feeling weak and therefore sought power, thus drawing her victimization into her expression of gender. How victimization connects to her feminine performance is obviously complicated, but Darowski draws the conclusion that "Her new body finally gave Betsy the fighting skills and endurance of her dreams. She was the object of both fear and desire" (*X-Men* 94). Thus, read in juxtaposition to her original presentation in *UXM* comics, the race-swapped Psylocke contributes a portrait of the unironic embodiment of Betsy's inner desire.

One issue after her transformation, Psylocke executes the five-person on-panel massacre described above. Interestingly, instead of portraying her state of mind as a killer as detached and zombielike, Claremont and penciler Jim Lee show a jubilant Psylocke gushing about her success. Hugging herself and smiling at the sky, she declares (almost juvenilely), "I won I won I won. For all their vaunted power, how easily I broke them to my master's will! How glorious the triumph feels!" (*I Am Lady Mandarin* 9). This rare eruption of emotion from the character stands in sharp contrast to the otherwise stoic Betsy whom the readers had gotten to know. This might be the happiest we have ever seen Psylocke, and she is surrounded by the bodies of her fallen victims.

All in all, Psylocke is a problematic character whose racial identity carries a layer of infamy that tends to dominate all discussions of her. However, as a piece of Claremont's broader subversion of gender roles, we might see in Psylocke a deeply gender-deviant portrayal that uses the concept of the feminine masquerade to reflect on the artificiality of female gender roles, thus adding something to the broader feminine cosmology of *UXM* comics through contrast and comparison.

This capacity to function more effectively as part of a broader ensemble of gender-subversive characters works particularly well when reading Betsy/Psylocke against Alison Blaire/Dazzler, who joins the series and the team at basically the same time. Alison is perhaps the most traditionally feminine *X-Men* character in the entire Claremont run. She's a former model/aerobics instructor/movie star/disco pop star. In the hands of pre-Claremont authors, Alison's true superpower might be the sheer number of her idealized hyperfeminine gender roles. Yet, despite this complicating history, Claremont is able to revitalize Alison as a character through the cultivation of her interior desire, and he eventually mobilizes the character within a compelling narrative commentary on toxic masculinity.

Although Alison/Dazzler made her comics debut briefly in the *Dark Phoenix Saga*, most of her backstory was created by Marvel comics editor-in-chief Jim Shooter with the help of many others who had intended to initially launch Dazzler as a transmedia superstar with a comic book, album, and a feature film starring Bo Derek—all simultaneously. These plans fizzled out, however, and Dazzler was left to settle for a bunch of guest spots in Marvel comics, followed by a forty-two-issue solo series, which Brian Johnson describes as an "extravagant celebration of romance comics and soap opera," and a "site of queer identification in the 1980s" (123).

Dazzler then became the subject of a graphic novel that picked up the soap opera thread but abandoned the queer subtext in favor of an objectifying, male-gaze-oriented portrayal. It is here that Alison's hyperfeminine nature is most directly established, in a graphic novel confusingly titled *Dazzler: The Movie* (Shooter et al.). The storyline has Alison striving to make it in Hollywood while navigating anti-mutant stigma, lecherous and exploitative men in positions of power, and her own nagging self-doubt. The issue features several male-gaze scenes, often involving Alison in a state of idealized undress. The graphic novel *Dazzler* is therefore described by Nicholas E. Miller as a book that "demonstrates a lack of self-awareness that tacitly condones the kinds of abusive behaviors it represents" (n.p.). All this is to say that Dazzler's performance of gender is very much aligned with the status quo, and Miller specifically singles out how the exploitative treatment Alison receives at the hands of powerful men goes completely uninterrogated.

Claremont picks up on this thread after Alison becomes an X-Woman in the wake of the *Mutant Massacre* storyline, in which Dazzler reluctantly joins the team for the sake of her own safety. From there, she becomes a character who speaks little, but who often shares her internal thought processes. According to our data, the only *X-Men* character with a higher thought:dialogue ratio is the secretive and pensive Rachel Summers. At the same time, Dazzler has a very high out-of-costume:in-costume ratio (fig. 3.3), despite having an established uniform throughout her time on the Claremont run (with the exception of her brief appearances post–Siege Perilous). This suggests that the character is frequently depicted in non-superhero-related scenes, something my reading strongly supports. We get to know Alison outside of her role in the X-Men quite frequently, thus offering a deeply

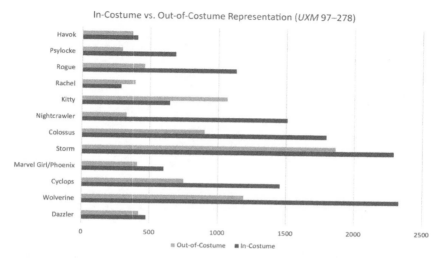

**Fig. 3.3.** *Number of in-costume versus out-of-costume depictions for each of Claremont's* X-Men *characters.*

humanized representation of the character that emphasizes her personal motivations and desires outside of being a superhero.

Dazzler is also declared dead on-panel four times (which is equal to Wolverine, who appears in more than three times as many panels). She is shown showering only once in the entirety of the run and never shown bathing, which speaks, perhaps, to sexualization, though she is definitely the subject of some so-called cheesecake shots during her time in *UXM* comics. All of this points to a character who exceeds expectations that she is performing a superficial damsel role.

A good example of this subversive potential comes, once again, in the issue titled *Lost in the Funhouse* (*UXM Annual* no. 11), where Dazzler's fantasy is genuinely harrowing and reveals her psychological complexity, thus humanizing her in a way that resists the male gaze around which so much of her pre-*X-Men* appearances seemed to orbit. In this same issue, which also features Betsy's skin-tearing reveal of the warrior underneath, Alison's desire comes through pluralistically, showing her visions of herself as a lawyer (she was a law student) and a rock star (her other career trajectory). Then a counterintuitive third option presents itself: it shows Alison as a homeless person rifling through a garbage bin. Trapped between three paths, she falls into a panic attack and crumples to her knees, noting that "If I never take a risk, I'll never have to worry about making a mistake, failing, being hurt. There's safety in defeat. Luxury in self-pity. Is

**Fig. 3.4.** *Alison contemplates her ideal life in* Lost in the Funhouse (UXM Annual, *vol. 1, no. 11). Alan Davis, penciler.*

that what I really want?" (26). And with that, she chooses to embody the homeless woman (fig. 3.4).

This scene reveals Alison's depth of character by adding new information about, or retconning, the overwhelming number of lives, goals, and roles she has had into a poignant meditation on the fundamental anxiety and insecurity that high-achieving people (perhaps women, specifically) carry with them as a burden. Here again it appears that Claremont is reinvigorating a female character who was ill-used by previous writers, just as he did with Jean Grey, Carol Danvers, and Psylocke.

Claremont again picks up this retcon thread in a storyline he composed for Alison that is a direct sequel to *Dazzler: The Movie* (Shooter et al.), one which critically interrogates the depiction of Alison in that book. In *Star 90* (*UXM* no. 260), Claremont directly explores the concept of toxic masculinity in sharp contrast to the male-gaze-affirming *Dazzler*. Claremont's title is a reference to the Bob Fosse film *Star 80* (1983), an adaptation of the Pulitzer Prize–winning essay "Death of a Playmate" by Teresa Carpenter, which chronicles the real-life murder of model Dorothy Stratten by her possessive and jealous husband. Thus, through intertextuality alone, Claremont establishes that the issue will feature a direct commentary on toxic masculinity within a superficial media culture.

The opening splash page features an image of Dazzler, seen through the crosshairs of a rifle, being shot in the chest. It is a violent and jarring start, but is quickly revealed to be misleading as the next page shows Eric Beale, a disgraced movie producer and her one-time paramour (in Shooter et al., *Dazzler*), who is here seen in full combat attire violently eviscerating a roomful of Dazzler mannequins (such as the one introduced on the splash page) while laughing maniacally and declaring, "Show that mutie witch in particular, you love Eric Beale, an' leave him, you pay the price" (3). The language here is telling, revealing the extent to which Eric feels ownership over Dazzler. It also shows that her status as a mutant is relevant only to reinforce the power relationship that Eric is imposing, especially his use of the term *witch*, which connects to an unlimited discourse of masculine anxiety about women in positions of power. Beale's backstory (as a creepy guy who went to preposterous lengths to pursue Alison) is told in *Dazzler* (Shooter et al.). It ends with Beale threatening to quash the movie unless Dazzler will sign a contract giving him complete control. After Beale tells her, "I will own you," she tears up the contract, thus giving up her dreams of stardom for the sake of her integrity (Shooter et al.).

The scene in *Star 90* immediately leaps to a different location "just up the coast" where Dazzler is caught in the possessive gaze of another man, Fred, who was introduced as an iconic nice guy in the previous issue. When Beale's production company goes under, Fred happens to buy the unreleased Dazzler movie at auction. He is himself a would-be movie producer whom we first see talking to a friend about feeling out of place at a "hotbod hotbox club so exclusively cool it doesn't have a name." He tells him it was "not my kinda place," to which his friend replies, "Fred, you wanna make the A-list, you gotta make the A-list scene." As he leaves, Fred retorts, "I'd rather make a good movie. Too many attitudes man. Everybody's playing games or running hustles." When he spots Alison at the bar on his way out, they connect, and she remarks, "Actually, you're the first person here who hasn't looked me over like a piece of fresh meat" (20), thus affirming Claremont's initial portrayal of Fred as an alternative to toxic masculinity.

Fred wants to market the Dazzler movie he purchased at auction, which will require Alison's involvement. Having lost her memories (courtesy of the Siege Perilous) and enjoying freedom from the limelight, Alison is patently uninterested and tells him, "I still don't understand what you want with me." The words that come to him appear in a thought bubble: "to think of me maybe the way I . . ."—just as Dazzler paddles out to sea on her surfboard, only to be targeted by Eric Beale with a sniper rifle (5). Beale's language reveals the extent of his obsession as he targets his prey:

> There she is oboy oboy oboy yeah soaring now warp speed totally focused crystal keen where oh where to place the bullet decisions decisions gut-shot so it's slow and agonizing or a head-shot instant obliteration smash the face yeah ruin those flawless features bye bye baybee. (6)

Here the absence of punctuation in Tom Orzechowski's lettering contributes to the portrayal of Beale as unhinged. Fred heroically rushes out to sea to save Alison and helps lead her to shore. Afterward, she agrees to promote the film as a way to flush her still-unknown stalker. This leads to a slapstick scene in which Beale tries to murder Dazzler on the studio lot but is mistaken for an actor entering wardrobe undressed. Staff members then put him in several different costumes (13–15).

This interlude has two potential effects. One is that it can be seen as diminishing the threat that Eric presents by portraying him as essentially harmless. Although that reading is possible in this slapstick scene, the opening and concluding scenes of the issue offer a much more severe and genuinely frightening tone. If this scene does normalize predatory behavior toward women, it is not representative of the overall tone of the story. We can read it as either an unfortunate inconsistency or an opportunity to ridicule the toxic male without diminishing the genuine threat that he represents.

Before the premiere of her movie, Dazzler walks alone on a beach in Malibu, reflecting on the extent to which her life is not her own.

> Should get a move on. Don't want to miss my gala premiere. Problem is, I don't much care. Is this what life's about? Acquiring all the toys money can buy? Was that why I was swept out of the sea from heaven knows where??? I know what people want and expect and demand of me but is that the real me? (19)

In this moment, Alison expresses the extent to which the relationship that her fans are forming with her is superficial in a way that reflects on the perceptions of both Fred and Eric.

Beale then attacks and kidnaps Alison, who wakes up in her original Dazzler costume with a bag over her face (again reflecting the extent to which Eric's attention is based purely on objectifying and fetishizing her). As she comes to, he approaches her with a sword, threatening, "Won't be long 'fore I splash that sleek skintight silver all nicely nice with scarlet yum." Again, the scene is remarkably dark for a Comics Code–era text and reestablishes the genuine threat/menace that Eric represents. Dazzler replies, "I don't know who you are, fella. Or why you've such a hate for me and to tell the truth I don't much care," as she fires lasers out of her eyes, sending Eric flying into a heap of dismembered Dazzler mannequins. He emerges soon after, proclaiming, "Give a man enough hate, be amazed at what he can do." Then they fight, a confrontation that emphasizes Alison's physical and mental prowess as a hero. As Eric approaches her with sword drawn, she hesitates to use lethal force, thinking, "Has to be another way! He's irrational, obsessed—impossible to reason with him." She decides to enact her code name and dazzle him instead, telling herself as she glows ever brighter,

> Don't think of his sword, focus on his pain, wash through the pain. There we go, that's the spirit. Breath deep and slow, Mr. Beale. Relax. There's nothing to be afraid of, no one here to hate. Flood him so full of beauty he can't bring himself to do it any harm.

This works. As a sobbing Eric begs her to stop, he declares, "I never imagined it was possible to behold such glory to feel so . . ." Dazzler interrupts, saying, "Only the first step down the road, Eric. Rest of the way, you'll have to go on your own" (20–23). And thus ends the issue.

This is Dazzler's exit from the Claremont run, but an important coda to the story can be found ten issues later when Fred shows up at the Malibu beach house looking for Alison. He is met by Dazzler's bodyguard (and future X-Man Guido), who explains that Alison doesn't live there anymore. Fred protests, "She can't do this! Especially to me. Her movie's top of the charts. She can't walk out on that kind of success! After all the work I put into the project—she owes me!" In response, Guido throws Fred into his car, then picks the car up with one hand and delivers what might be the ultimate moral of the story:

> You gotta seriously terminal attitude. Fact is, the lady didn't want 'cher help or ask for it. An' you sure aint sufferin' cause a what 'chu did, am I right? Italian suits, Italian cars, major production deals up the wazoo. Sittin' in the cat bird seat, my man. Most'd be satisfied wid a fraction of that but nnnnnnoooo you gotta have yerself a

trophy-babe! You gotcher life, sport. Let Dazzler enjoy hers. You may figure her to be your talisman but you can't possess her any more'n 'at creep Eric Beale could. (*X-Tinction Agenda: First Strike* 13–14)

This juxtaposition between the two men hammers home the message of toxic masculinity and the extent to which men can develop possessive attitudes toward women, in part as an expression of their masculinity. Even to Fred, Alison was an object, and juxtaposing him with an over-the-top stalker like Eric Beale aligns his obviously toxic behavior with the nice-guy behavior we see in Fred. In all of this, Claremont depicts Alison as a victim of her own sexual appeal, rendered vulnerable within a patriarchal system that commodifies her and encourages both violence and possessiveness toward her. That Claremont is able to tell this story through the vehicle of a character who once functioned that exact way in her previous comics appearances is perhaps his greatest accomplishment in subverting gender roles. In Claremont's hands, Dazzler effectively subverts Dazzler.

As a finale to this discussion of later-run X-Women, I would like to highlight *Ladies Night* (*UXM* no. 244) as an example of an issue that brings a lot of Claremont's subversions of gender roles into a more farcical environment. It also shines a direct spotlight on the shared feminine community of the X-Women in particular, even as it speaks to the artificiality of isolated gender rituals.

The tone is set by the cover of the issue, with art by Mark Silvestri and Dan Green, showing the four X-Women in unfamiliar cowering postures as shadows loom over them. They lament, "No!," "We've survived Inferno," "Beaten Freedom Force, the Sentinels, and Magneto!," "But how do we beat *gasp* the M Squad!" (*Ladies Night*). This sets the essential sarcastic tone of the story to come, but also its more complex subversion of gender tropes. The X-Women can be seen to perform the damsel-in-distress type so familiar to comics readers (the feminine masquerade again), although here readers' knowledge of the X-Women's characters immediately establishes the irony that drives the issue. Readers who are even remotely familiar with the characters know that the X-Women Storm, Rogue, Psylocke, and Dazzler do not cower the way they do on this cover.

Inside, the issue opens by introducing us to Jubilee, Claremont's last new X-Woman. She is first seen living in a Hollywood shopping mall and using her mutant powers to busk for money. Through this vocation, she earns the ire of mall security, and they hire the M Squad, a mutant-hunting quartet parodically based on the Ghostbusters, to deal with her. The story then cuts to the Outback, where tensions among Rogue, Storm, Dazzler, and Psylocke are running high in the aftermath of the darkly tragic *Inferno* storyline from the previous issue. Dazzler proposes a solution in the form of a dramatic monologue: "Storm, being X-Men is who we are, defending mutantkind and the world, what we do, but does it have to be every minute of every day? There has to be time off for ourselves, y'know, so the rest of it has meaning." Storm asks if she has a solution, and Dazzler replies, "You bet. Let's take an evening off. Let's indulge ourselves and go somewhere exciting. Let's be footloose and fancy free, girls. Let's have fun! Let's go shopping!" (12).

The tone here is nuanced. Claremont is exploring the juxtaposition between the superficiality of the solution that Dazzler is offering and the existential nature of the problem. At the same time, the solution is posed by his most consumerist character, who is advocating here a literal validation of retail therapy. And the fact that Dazzler is leading the way establishes the most effective gender commentary of the issue by looking at a culturally established feminine ritual through the eyes of a spectrum of feminine characters, with the most feminine of the four leading the way as the others follow with varying degrees of reluctance.

When they arrive at the mall, the X-Women immediately catch the attention of Jubilee, who looks at them enviously for their confidence and power, and then their physical appearance: "They're so—beautiful! I wish . . . I wish . . . not a prayer" (14), thus establishing the X-Women as feminine idols. From there, Claremont indulges in a bit of camp as Dazzler leads her reluctant teammates through a series of feminine rituals, including haircuts, makeovers, and shopping for clothes and shoes. The camp element is best established by an exchange with Storm, who asks, "Why must I paint my face?" Dazzler replies, "To look good." Storm asks, "Why?" Dazzler responds, "So people'll look at you." Storm says, "They already do too often. I do not like it." At that point, Psylocke interjects, saying, "Stop being so serious, Storm. This is play!" (15).

This again returns to the feminine masquerade (and, appropriately, it is Psylocke who demonstrates awareness of the concept); these women, from all walks of life, are playfully embodying a gender role that is ineffectively one-size-fits-all for the sake of having fun. Furthermore, the fact that the issue places so much emphasis on the challenges of constructing images of femininity (all the labor required to select an outfit, apply makeup, style their hair, and so on) gives rise to the sense of the artifice of the performance. It takes an absurd amount of work to embody the feminine ideal. We should also note, of course, that Jubilee identified their beauty before they undertake this laborious transformation.

At this point (in an iconic two-panel sequence) Dazzler declares, "All right ladies, now that we're dressed to kill, let's party!" From there, they go to a Chippendales bar where Alison bribes the host to have a dancer pull Storm onto the stage with him. Alison calls from the crowd, "Don't be a weenie, boss!," while Psylocke adds, "Remember, Storm—play!" (16–18). Storm does and eventually appears to enjoy herself, and her teammates watching from the table do as well.

Then the M-Squad attacks, and the X-Women jump into action, protecting a young mutant from a society that fears and hates them all just for being mutants, a mission that the four women execute efficiently and effectively (thus reminding us of their heroic pedigrees). This juxtaposition between play and superheroic feats emphasizes the compatibility of the feminine rituals and the heroes' mission. This point is driven home by Jubilee, who repeatedly expresses admiration for their feminine aesthetic and their heroic power and agency. Her decision to follow them home through their portal, to become one of them, eventually and essentially is a clear testament to the endorsement of their paradigmatic function—the simple, fundamental notion being that the X-Women are heroes that a young girl can look up to. They have inspired Jubilee.

In that sense, what we see in *Ladies Night* reflects what we see throughout Claremont's interrogation of feminine gender roles during his run: a variety of characters conforming to gender roles to varying degrees and in ways that do not masculinize or undervalue specific feminine traits, while at the same time intersecting with a wide variety of social categories depending on the background of each individual (heavy emphasis on "individual"). All of this is wrapped up in characters who openly challenge the normalization of gender roles in ways that vary from complex undermining to the simple act of portraying female characters with agency, power, and relatability.

# CHAPTER 4

# She Makes Him Nervous

*Cyclops's Baseline Masculinity and the Exchange of Gender Power*

My image of [Scott Summers] was more like a very young Henry Fonda. Very Nebraska, very mid-Atlantic; middle-class is right. Middle America is better. Yet with surprising sidelines to his personality, again like Fonda.

—CHRIS CLAREMONT, FROM A COMIC MEDIA NEWS INTERVIEW

Although Claremont's progressive portrayals of female characters are firmly entrenched in the author's legacy, his portrayals of male characters are less discussed. The first thing to note is that his portrayal of masculinity is simpatico with his portrayals of the female characters described in earlier chapters; indeed, the gender portrayals of the male characters depend quite intimately on their relationships with the compelling and powerful female characters they fight alongside.

This interplay has been noted by Carol Cooper in a pair of prominent ways. In the first, she observes that powerful male characters in *X-Men* comics are often willing to accept subservient roles in relationship to more powerful female characters—that these men "humbly applied to be consorts of women they clearly considered superior to themselves" (197). This dynamic has been discussed in previous chapters but is also clearly reflected in Cyclops's relationship to Jean Grey after she transforms into Phoenix (the main subject of this chapter).

The other prominent effect of the X-Women on the X-Men is more complex, relying upon the fundamental leadership role and its effect on subordinates.

One unexpected side benefit of showing females as leaders is how their less impassive demeanour makes it okay for men to show emotional warmth, doubt, vulnerability, and other qualities that might otherwise be considered unproductively effeminate. Even berserker characters like Magneto and Wolverine have gradually revealed more human and redemptive sides of themselves upon prolonged exposure to women like Jean and Storm. (Cooper 197)

This applies to the fundamental rank system imposed on the X-Men under Storm as their leader (and, later, very briefly, Psylocke), but also to more subtle hierarchies, such as Phoenix's unacknowledged role as team leader by virtue of her power and abilities, even when she was not technically calling the shots. Either way, the series shows men who were not just taking orders from women, but also learning from them and, through this process, allowing gender-deviant aspects of their own personalities to come forward in imitation of the women inspiring them. It therefore stands to reason that any cohesive patterns of gender representation in the series are the product of this push and pull between the opposing extremes of the social category of gender. These extremes are rendered (canonically) as a binary, and the intersections are once again many, so it makes sense to start this portion of my inquiry with a closer look at the male character who best embodies the social norms of hegemonic masculinity and who also happens to embrace many key roles that are central to the conception of that same hegemonic masculinity.[1]

Scott Summers (aka Cyclops) is one of the most iconic characters in *X-Men* history. Raised an orphan, Scott did not develop his mutant powers properly because of a childhood injury he suffered in the catastrophic plane crash that cost him his parents. He has the power to shoot concussive-force beams from his eyes, but he cannot control them without the aid of a ruby visor. His childhood in a Nebraska orphanage was tragic, but when Professor X offered him new purpose as a member of the X-Men team, Scott came into his own.

The idea of a symbolic push and pull between subversive representations of femininity and masculinity is effectively embodied in the figure of Scott/Cyclops, whose undermining of masculine gender roles is particularly dependent on his reactions to the progressive (and progressing) representation of Jean/Phoenix as she transitions from trophy object to goddess (as discussed in depth in chapter 1). In this chapter I explore how the character of Cyclops personifies broader cultural anxieties about paradigmatic shifts in a patriarchal culture. He is the alpha male leader of the team and perfectly embodies what Audre Lorde refers to as "the mythical norm" (633), but he becomes anxious and threatened when Jean, his girlfriend, achieves a previously unfathomable level of power as Phoenix.[2] How Cyclops negotiates his agency within both the relationship dynamic and the leadership hierarchy of the X-Men symbolizes and personifies broader cultural paradigm shifts with regard to the concept of masculinity and gives a unique popular culture voice to the specific anxieties that those shifts were creating in society.

Cyclops's embodiment of white masculinity at the time Claremont took over the character is, to Neil Shyminsky, nearly absolute: "Cyclops's whiteness does not register as a particular race so much as a lack of race. We are far more aware of what he is not—not black like Storm, not Jewish like Kitty Pryde—rather than what he *is*, and so he can be perceived as simply a human" ("Mutation, Racialization, Decimation" 161). This conformity to the established in-group makes Scott/Cyclops a useful starting point for our exploration of male gender roles in *UXM*, but it also connects the character to a tradition of pop culture representations of white masculinity.

As discussed by scholar Megan Abbott, white masculinity in American popular culture has often been defined as a struggle against ongoing social paradigm shifts—a sort of heroic conservatism amidst changing values. In describing the noir hero of the 1930s–1950s, Abbott notes that the "idea of the solitary white man trekking down urban streets has forerunners in like-minded navigators of Western space or wilderness" (2) and is therefore a logical extension of an ongoing cultural portrayal of white masculinity. For Abbott, the noir hero is more specifically defined by contextual anxieties such as "depression-era fears about a capitalism-defeated masculinity, anti-immigrant paranoia, Cold War xenophobia, and the grip of post–World War II consumerism" (2).

Cyclops debuted in 1963 in *UXM* no. 1, the first *X-Men* issue, titled simply *X-Men* (Lee and Kirby), but Claremont remodeled him in the Fonda-esque middle-American tradition in the 1970s, a time when cultural anxieties still included immigrant paranoia (foregrounded in Claremont's handling of the international X-Men team that Cyclops became the leader of). For our purposes, however, the far more relevant anxiety is what Shyminsky, in his reading of *X-Men*, refers to as "a recent 'crisis' in white masculinity" ("Mutant Readers" 393) resulting from the destabilization of the social category of "man" by feminism. Yet rather than portraying Cyclops in the conservative white, masculine tradition identified by Abbott, Claremont instead built his Cyclops around a slow-dawning, deeply difficult acceptance of the new masculinity that Shyminsky identifies, one that eschews the long-established celebration of hypermasculine extremes associated with hegemonic masculinity.

In the earliest days of *X-Men* comics, long before Claremont's arrival, Cyclops's conformity to hegemonic masculinity is constructed through two ongoing conflicts: the internal competition among his male teammates for the affection of Jean Grey, and the internal competition among his male teammates for affection and validation from their male patriarch, Professor X. Within each of these competitions exists a long-established (ancient even) paradigm of defining masculinity through external validation.

On the very first page of *X-Men* (Lee and Kirby), Charles Xavier (aka Professor X), the unchallenged patriarch of the X-Men family, summons the team for the first time. He does not use the iconic "To me, my X-Men" line, but rather the less jingoistic "Attention, X-Men, this is Professor Xavier calling. Repeat: this is Professor X calling. You are ordered to appear at once. Tardiness will be punished." The first to answer is Cyclops: "Cyclops present and accounted for, Sir!" (1). This scene sets the tone for the portrayal of Cyclops as Xavier's most loyal subordinate and most devoted follower throughout the series.

By issue no. 7 (Lee, *The Return of the Blob*), Cyclops receives his atonement from the father, so to speak, when Xavier names him leader of the X-Men. "I have decided that you, the X-Man known as Cyclops, shall be group leader until I return." Cyclops expresses immediate shock at the revelation. "Me?? But, Sir—the Beast is a better scholar—while Angel is more aggressive, and—!" Xavier cuts him off midsentence, saying, "But it is you who possess the rare quality of leadership! My decision stands" (Lee, *The Return of the Blob* 7).

Xavier's favoritism of Cyclops conveys a form of patrilineal approval in which Cyclops exchanges his individual agency (and any sort of rebelliousness associated with being a teenager) for the position of prominence among his peers, a position he earns through supplication to the dream and demands of Charles Xavier. Cyclops had already been the group's strongest proponent of Xavier's dream, and, as the series progresses, he continues to carry that burden more often than any of the other X-Men. As leader, Cyclops operates as a proxy for Xavier's patriarchal power, keeping the team in line and on task with Xavier's demands. In doing so, Cyclops is rewarded with an alpha male position within the *X-Men* universe, a position that is further validated when Jean settles on him as her romantic partner. This is who Scott/Cyclops was when Claremont inherited the character.

As Gerri Mahn notes in his reading of hegemonic masculinity in *X-Men* comics, "the 1970s saw a rise in the academic recognition of masculinity as a social construct and of a power dynamic differentiating 'normative' from 'non-normative' types of behavior," creating what he identifies as a "crisis of masculinity" (117). Context is again important here. As Mahn observes, "Gender was a driving force for comic book narratives since the medium was specifically innovated in 1933 for a male demographic" (116). Thus, once *X-Men* comics became the best-selling superhero comics in the industry, having the alpha male team leader exhibiting nonnormative types of behavior represents a momentous shift from an established and highly prominent site for the production of hegemonic masculinity. In this sense, Cyclops's potential for subversion of gender roles was restricted by the standards of the time, and all the more significant as a result.

While the other original X-Men depart to live new lives in *UXM* no. 94, *The Doomsmith Scenario!* (Claremont), Scott/Cyclops decides to stay with the new team, recognizing that his identity is inextricable from his role as leader of the X-Men (thus initiating Cyclops's first longstanding character arc throughout the Claremont run).[3] "I'm an X-Man pure and simple," he tells a bereft Jean. "This is my home, my life. This is where I . . . belong" (5). The separation of Scott and Jean (she leaves the series at this point) places the relationship politics predominantly off-panel, thus pushing Jean's capacity to serve as a sexual trophy off-panel as well. Moreover, from this point on, Claremont will continue to cultivate Scott's gradual (and painful) development of an existence defined outside of his role as leader of the X-Men, undermining the masculine stereotype of self-martyrdom and emotional detachment. In an interview, Claremont explained that "for me, for Scott, it was all about real life" (Claremont, interview with Astrid Sparks).

The first major event to spur Cyclops's disengagement from the leadership role is the death of Thunderbird in the next issue, titled *Warhunt!* (*UXM* no. 95). Building on Len Wein and Dave Cockrum's aggressively macho portrayal of Cyclops in *Giant-Size X-Men* no. 1, Claremont exaggerates those features to the point of a critical failing. During their first training event, the narrator tells the reader, "And when they falter, give in a little, give up, a voice snaps them back into line. A harsh voice, angry, biting, merciless. The voice of the man named Cyclops, who drives the X-Men hard and himself harder" (*The Doomsmith Scenario!* 6). But from this point forward, Claremont portrays Cyclops's "drive" not as heroic, but as innately destructive to his sense of well-being.

After Thunderbird dies on the new X-Men's first mission (under Cyclops's leadership), the next issue (*UXM* no. 96) opens with a famous bit of narration. While Cyclops wanders the grounds of the mansion, Claremont's narrator takes on a life of its own, chiding Scott for his failure:

Autumn's come early this year—the September apples hanging heavy in the orchards, the trees on both sides of the Hudson river ablaze with a thousand myriad fires, a thousand myriad shades of . . . death! You know him well, don't you, Cyclops—this dark one, this great destroyer—you and your fellow X-Men have walked with him all your young lives—flaunted him, taunted him, tilted with him—and you'd always gotten away unscathed . . . until now. Until . . . Thunderbird. It's been weeks now since Thunderbird died, and the memory still hurts, doesn't it, Cyclops? . . . The nagging feeling—the fear—that if you'd acted differently, Thunderbird would be alive today. Awake or asleep you can't escape the images seared into your mind's eye! Images of Count Nefaria making a desperate attempt to flee Valhalla Base . . . of Thunderbird trying to stop him . . . of Thunderbird's final defiant cry! You remember what happened next, don't you, Cyclops? And what happened after that? Thunderbird hadn't gotten out. That's the real hell of his death, isn't it, Cyclops—because you know he hadn't even tried to get out. You and the X-Men had saved the world from a nuclear holocaust—but you'd lost a man to do it . . . and try as you might, you can't balance those scales in your mind or in your heart . . . can you, Cyclops? Can you? Can you?! (*Night of the Demon!* 1–3)

Scott comforts himself by accepting this as the burden of being an X-Man in general and, in particular, the team's leader. But here Claremont is expressing his major thematic stance on leadership—one that he likewise used to build a character arc around Storm: the alpha position is innately undesirable and emotionally damaging. Cyclops begins to recognize that in this scene, and that dawning awareness will continue to define his character throughout Claremont's run.

By *UXM* no. 98, Scott and Jean's relationship is reestablished after being left somewhat uncertain in the wake of Jean leaving the team. Importantly, Jean initiates the couple's first kiss. After years of "Will they or won't they?," Scott is seen thinking aloud about X-Men problems when Jean interrupts him: "Stop it! It's Christmas, Scott—and you've been tearing yourself apart over Alex [Cyclops's brother, who has turned into a villain] for weeks. Can't you just this once give it a rest and kiss me. Didn't you hear me, you big lug—I said kiss me" (*Merry Christmas, X-Men* 2–3). She then kisses him as he mumbles in protest. Appropriately, this action occurs directly in front of cartoon renderings of Jack Kirby and Stan Lee, who created the characters. Claremont even has them express shock at the differing politics on display. Kirby remarks, "I tell ya, they never used to do that when we had the book" (3). This observation is apt for a series that used to leave Jean in a permanent state of longing (and being longed for). As scholar Christy Marx notes, however, Jean achieves a greater sense of agency when her relationship with Cyclops is "allowed to deepen and actually go somewhere" (174). What we see in this scene is the beginning of that development, as Scott and Jean finally affirm their love for each other, just before the Sentinels (giant robots dedicated to the destruction of the mutant species) show up and abduct Jean, setting in motion the events that will lead to her transformation into Phoenix.

The mechanics of the issue also amplify the conflict between Cyclops's sense of duty and his desire to cultivate a domestic existence for himself as Scott. The issue presents a sort of domestic juxtaposition by giving Cyclops a rare moment of happiness, and giving it to him outside of his uniform, as the X-Men are all in civilian attire at this point. His kiss with Jean occurs only after he splits apart from the group, again creating a sense of the benefit of removing himself from the X-Men context. Furthermore, the fact that his moment of happiness with Jean is interrupted by an attack at the hands of iconic *X-Men* villains further reflects the conflict between Scott Summers's self-actualization as a person and the dehumanizing effect of his role as Cyclops, leader of the X-Men: his moment with Jean is literally interrupted by X-Men obligations, aggressively and violently.

After the conflict with the Sentinels is resolved, Claremont presents a scene that clearly indicates the extent to which Cyclops's priorities are shifting. When Jean offers to martyr herself to save the team (as they are escaping from the Sentinels' space station), Cyclops's response is uncharacteristically extreme, bordering on hysterical. He shakes her violently, and even starts to insult her: "And how will you survive the solar flare, you little—!" (*Greater Love Hath No X-Man* 27). Jean, in sharp contrast to Cyclops's hysterics, is perfectly calm and rational, acting more like Cyclops than Cyclops himself. It is also here that Jean pulls rank on him, knocking him out so that he can no longer hinder her mission of self-sacrifice.

Jean's actions offer a compelling contrast to some very old gender roles seen in Western literature, including those advanced by Virgil in the *Aeneid*. As classicist Helen Lovatt notes in her analysis of the gender divide in the archetypal Dido/Aeneas relationship, the parallel characters, each conflicted between public responsibility and personal love, are ultimately separated by gender roles and the expectations that they create. Lovatt observes that "becoming part of the story is a step too far for femininity, a step from epic into tragedy, across the boundaries of genre. Dido's public speeches show that she is a match and a mirror for Aeneas, yet remains distinctly feminine" (n.p.). Although Aeneas honors his duty, Dido abandons hers in a dramatic display of what is "expected of women: self-pitying, over-emotional, hysterical" (Lovatt n.p.). This classical paradigm was still in existence when Claremont scripted his scene. Connell acknowledges that "a familiar theme in patriarchal ideology is that men are rational while women are emotional" (164). However, that theme is inverted in Claremont's scene, with Jean acting rationally and selflessly while Scott is the one in hysterics—the one who would sacrifice everything for love, even his duty.

This scene also provides an important contrast to the Scott/Jean relationship from earlier issues of *X-Men* comics. Joseph Darowski, in his analysis of pre-Claremont Jean Grey, recognizes that "though Marvel Girl's powers are an asset, she frequently is too physically weak to use them or a man must direct her because she is too emotionally frail" (*X-Men* 49). In this sense, Jean's insubordination toward her hysterical leader/boyfriend is an assertion of agency, allowing her to claim—perhaps for the first time—absolute authority over her powers and use them, to their utmost, outside of the control of a patriarchal figure, saving the lives of everyone else in the process.

When Cyclops awakens inside the life cell of the ship, he becomes hysterical again. With Kurt and Piotr holding him back, he screams, "Let me go, blast you! Let me go to her before it's too late. . . . Please, Kurt, I beg you—please" (*Greater Love Hath No X-Man* 31). Claremont's emotional and irrational Cyclops offers a poignant counter-portrayal to what we saw at the outset of the Claremont run, as well as in previous iterations of the character. Where the old Cyclops would do whatever it takes to accomplish a mission, this one is capable of valuing love over his leadership role. It is a stark shift in the character's preestablished (highly gendered) priorities and further sets Scott/Cyclops on a path toward the cultivation of a richer personal life.

In the very next issue (*UXM* no. 101), Jean is in a coma, and Claremont presents Scott in the hospital waiting room contemplating how he himself has changed.

> All those wasted years . . . when I loved Jean and she loved me and neither of us had the sense to tell the other . . . and now, if she dies, it'll have all been for nothing. I mean, what do you do when the light goes out of your life? When Jean moved down to the city to build a life for herself outside the X-Men, I let her go because I thought . . . that the X-Men were what gave my life meaning. But they're not. It's

> Jean. It's always been Jean, only I never realized it 'til now when I'm
> about to lose her forever. (*Like a Phoenix, from the Ashes* 14)

Scott's rejection of the validity of his leadership role is then appropriately demonstrated in terms of its impact on his patrilineal relationship to Professor X/Xavier. In *UXM* no. 102, Xavier informs Scott (who is still watching over Jean in the hospital) that the X-Men have been ambushed by the villainous Juggernaut, and Scott must go and lend his assistance. He refuses, choosing instead to stay with Jean. Xavier is outraged: "You're what?! You're putting the life of one woman ahead of your fellow X-Men?!" "I am," Scott says. "Because that woman is the most important thing in my life." Xavier becomes further incensed, thus highlighting the extent of what he sees as betrayal: "How dare you!?! You ungrateful, unspeakable cur! I took you in!" (*Who Will Stop the Juggernaut?* 17). The simple point here is that Scott is reconfiguring his priorities and roles. Because those roles were established in previous comics through archetypal masculine challenges and paradigms, Scott's rejection of them, and the subsequent invalidation of their worth, can be read as gender subversive.

After Jean's release from the hospital, Scott's first glimpse of her new power comes in *UXM* no. 105, in which he thinks to himself, "My . . . God. Jean used to be the weakest X-Man. Now she powers up an inter-stellar transporter without batting an eyelash" (*Phoenix Unleashed!* 30). Interestingly, this is the same issue that features Jean's battle with Firelord, which, as described in chapter 1, has important symbolic ramifications. Dave Cockrum has said that in order to subvert Jim Shooter's mandate that a female character could not be allowed to defeat Silver Surfer or Thor, Claremont had Phoenix win a battle against Firelord, a former herald of Galactus and a character who, as Cockrum notes, had previously beaten both Thor and the Silver Surfer. Thus Scott's uncomfortable acknowledgment of Jean/Phoenix's power comes at a time when Claremont and Cockrum were specifically subverting the gender expectations of the editorial department.

Another incident in which Scott is intimidated by Jean's power shows up in *UXM* no. 109. After witnessing Phoenix stitch together the fabric of reality itself, Scott is again left shaken and reflecting on how she has changed. When Jean's parents arrive to talk with her, Scott asks, "Jean, d'you want me to come along?" But she refuses him, noting that they would rather be alone. Scott is left standing, watching Jean and her parents walk through a doorway. In a scene that is perhaps reminiscent of the final scene of Francis Ford Coppola's film *The Godfather*, he asks aloud,

"But what about you and me, Jean? When are we going to talk?" (*Home Are the Heroes!* 7). Of course, she has already left, spatially symbolizing the distance that has come between them, and the effect that distance has on their ability to communicate.

Scott then retreats to brood in the mansion's study, watching out the window as Jean reveals her new Phoenix form to her parents. His mood is obviously sour; when Kurt/Nightcrawler checks in on him, he makes a snide remark about Kurt's circus background. Kurt thinks, "Such bitterness in his voice—I have never heard its like from Scott before" (*Home Are the Heroes!* 14). Given the power dynamic, Scott taking out his frustration on Kurt reflects his sense of impotence, which leads him to abuse his leadership position to feel powerful again. In the next issue he again reflects on Jean's detachment, thinking to himself, "Blast it, woman, I want to help you! Why won't you talk to me anymore?!" (*The "X"-Sanction* 31). In these instances, it is evident that Scott is struggling with the transition of power in his relationship with Jean.

Shortly after this, the pair are once again separated, with each left to believe that the other has been killed. Both of them move on. Jean travels to move past her grief, while Scott reflects on how he doesn't really feel the grief at all (perhaps as a result of Jean's transformation to Phoenix). He actually moves on by starting what appears to be a romantic relationship with Colleen Wing (a martial artist that Claremont included in the previously written *Iron Fist*). However, this relationship never advances (though Colleen does offer Scott a key to her apartment).

Jean/Phoenix and Scott/Cyclops are reunited in *UXM* no. 126. Cyclops even breaks ranks in a combat situation in order to run to her: "I'm breaking my own rules by taking off on my own into a potential danger area. But after all that's happened I want to be alone when I see Jean." The narrator tells us, "With each step, the emotions he's dammed up for so long threaten to bust wide open. He knows he must lock them down, or break. He thought she was the woman he loved . . . but now . . .?" (*How Sharper Than a Serpent's Tooth . . . !* 10).

That question will be forestalled by an enduring battle with the reality-altering mutant Proteus, but after that, the couple have a conversation to clear the air. In *UXM* no. 129, Scott tells Jean that Colleen was "a friend"—that he had turned his emotions off when he thought Jean was dead because the pain of losing her was just too great. He proclaims, "Jean, you're everything to me—as necessary as the air I breathe. I used to say 'I love you' without truly knowing what I was talking about. I know now—a little, anyway. Jean—I love you." She responds, "And I, you, Scott. With all my heart" (*God Spare the Child . . .* 9). In this instance, Scott's transition from callous stoicism to emotional eruption and declaration of dependency upon Jean serves as a poignant microcosm for his broader anxiety about being vulnerable within their relationship. When he thought Jean was dead, he "dammed up" his emotions, but he is unable to maintain the emotional stoicism that Connell identifies as a key aspect of hegemonic masculinity (131–133).

This same issue also features Scott's biggest confrontation with Professor X/Xavier up to this point, with Scott openly challenging Xavier's authority by questioning his strategy regarding mentorship of the new X-Men. As in the scene with Jean, Scott gains a moment of epiphany from this encounter: "This is crazy! To him, I'm still the untried kid who's allowed only so much responsibility with the X-Men and no more!" (*God Spare the Child . . .* 14). Again, we see parallel developments in these two aspects of Scott's previously established masculine validation mechanisms. As one crumbles, so does the other, and instead of Scott falling apart in consequence of either symbolic demolition, Claremont's character may actually be growing as a person.

Unfortunately for Scott, the *Dark Phoenix Saga*, the *X-Men*'s most famous and beloved storyline, is now underway. He spends the early issues marveling at Jean/Phoenix's power with each subsequent escalation, eventually thinking in *UXM* no. 131, "I should be proud of her—instead, I'm frightened" (*Run for Your Life!* 16). On the literal level, fear of an all-powerful cosmic being is quite rational, but on the symbolic level, we again see a progressively diminishing alpha male becoming more and more insecure about his relationship with, and to, a powerful woman. All of this will come to a climax in *UXM* no. 132, in which Claremont uses the sexual dynamic of Jean's relationship with Scott to explore and explicate the broader symbolic relationship between the two that has been unfolding in previous issues.

In *And Hellfire Is Their Name!* (*UXM* no. 132) (discussed from Jean's perspective in chapter 1), Scott is holding a strategy meeting on top of a butte in the middle of nowhere with another original X-Man, Warren Worthington/Angel, when Jean arrives with a picnic basket. The fact that she specifically intrudes on a strategy meeting is telling of her emerging sense of agency and her willingness to disrupt this masculinist ritual, which she had been excluded from quite deliberately. Scott had previously asked Warren if they could speak somewhere private—consciously excluding Jean and the other X-Men.

Jean's assertion of her agency in this scene is enhanced by her effectively shooing Angel away and asserting an agenda in direct contradiction to that of Scott. "Someone mention my name? You fellas have been talking for hours. Time for a break" (*And Hellfire Is Their Name!* 6). Enhancing the matter even further is the fact that—at the exact moment of Jean's arrival—Scott is interrupted from discussing her behind her back. He had been saying to Warren, "And, as if that wasn't enough to worry about, something odd has been happening to Jean lately" (6), but Jean arrives before he can finish that thought. The two briefly reflect on how Warren has "grown up," at which point Jean transforms her costume into a revealing two-piece, saying, "We've all grown up, Scott" (7). The juxtaposition of text and image creates a double entendre, with Jean's revealing outfit tied to the concept of maturation, a reading that is justified through the soon-to-be-revealed fact that she is there to seduce Scott. The dialogue also, however, highlights the idea of Jean's progression and evolution into Phoenix, suggesting that Phoenix is a grown-up version of Jean, a more mature and empowered version—her best self (fig. 4.1).

Instead of celebrating that, Scott becomes uncomfortable, thinking to himself, "She did it again, changed from costume to street clothes by telekinetically rearranging the molecules of her outfit. Why do I find that so disconcerting? Why shouldn't Jean use her psi-powers to make her life easier?" (*And Hellfire Is Their Name!* 7). His pensive response is reflective of his progression as a character. Scott is aware that he has no right to feel uncomfortable about Jean's use of her power, and yet he does. This can easily be read as intuition about the dark events that are soon to come, but metaphorically this can be read as a brief moment of insight into his own internal struggle to accept the rational notion of an empowered woman, even as longstanding hierarchies and powers leave him feeling anxious about the concept. Thus, in this scene, Scott can again be seen to personify the crisis of masculinity that Mahn speaks about (117). Scott wants to be progressive, but he still feels uncomfortable subverting the gender roles that had previously defined his relationship with Jean.

Jean then goes a step further in her exercise of power and authority, pulling off Cyclops's visor without his consent. Given the dense sexual symbolism of Cyclops's visor as a signifier of sublimated "erotic energies" (Bukatman 56) and the enhanced sexual context of the scene unfolding, this action can be seen as an assertion of sexual dominance, as is Jean's newly revealed power to hold back Scott's optic blasts while they make love, controlling his symbolic eruption in a manner that can be read as analogous to sexual domination. Even as Scott embraces her (on a pastoral butte with the sunset behind them), he cannot stop feeling insecure. "I don't believe it! My eyes—how can Jean hold back all that power." He tries

**Fig. 4.1.** *Jean Grey seduces Scott Summers in* And Hellfire Is Their Name! *(UXM, vol. 1, no. 132). John Byrne, penciler.*

to speak, "Jean . . . ," but is yet again interrupted and controlled. "Hush," she says. "No questions now, my love. No words" (*And Hellfire Is Their Name!* 7). This is the final panel of the scene. We should perhaps note that the use of "hush" has infantilizing connotations here as well. Jean is completely in control.

From there, the *Dark Phoenix Saga* unfolds through symbols of sexual competition between Scott/Cyclops and his rival Jason Wyngarde/ Mastermind, who seeks to seduce Jean through telepathic illusion. Appropriately, Cyclops and Mastermind cross swords over Jean's affections in a hallucinatory mindscape. The phallic sword imagery here is obvious and adds another dimension to Cyclops's anxiety over symbolic emasculation. In *UXM* issue no. 133, Claremont plays into this anxiety further by having Cyclops fare quite poorly in the duel, being openly taunted by Mastermind and then easily defeated. Emasculated again, Cyclops lies prone on the ground in the real world and is even mistakenly declared dead by his teammate Nightcrawler (*Wolverine: Alone!* 30). By participating in traditional masculine rituals of violent and phallic competition for Jean's affections, Cyclops is defeated utterly. It is only by deviating from such hypermasculine rituals that he has any hope of completing his mission.

In the next issue (no. 134), *Too Late, the Heroes!*, we learn that Cyclops was hurt quite badly in the duel, yet instead of giving Cyclops another chance to defeat Mastermind, who had just emasculated him in front of his girlfriend, Claremont has Jean/Phoenix take on Mastermind solo. Like the duel between Mastermind and Cyclops, this one is not much of a contest. Phoenix is in complete control and easily eliminates the threat that Mastermind presents after using her powers to free Cyclops from his captivity. As this transpires, Cyclops thinks, "I can hear her, feel her. She's so beautiful—shining like a star" (6). In this moment, Cyclops has appreciation for the beauty of Phoenix's power instead of feeling threatened by it. From there, the team defeats Mastermind and the Hellfire Club.

Unfortunately, things go bad thereafter, with the damage done to Jean/Phoenix's psyche taking its toll and transforming her into Dark Phoenix (as discussed in chapter 1). She ultimately takes her life in front of Cyclops in order to safeguard the world from her power. In response, he resigns from the X-Men to grieve and pursue a life outside of his duty to the team. Miles Booy refers to this move as "the most audacious shift in line-up" during Claremont's tenure and the culmination of Scott/Cyclops's character's arc (110–111). From a broad perspective, Scott comes to perceive the toxic nature of his relationship with the X-Men and embraces the necessity of building a life that is antithetical to the boyhood masculinist fantasy of leading a superhero team—a fantasy that was specifically commodified for comics readers in Cyclops's pre-Claremont characterization.

Scott then travels, falls in love, and eventually has a child. During this era, he is portrayed as unburdened, self-invested, and ultimately quite happy. He becomes a more emotional and physically affectionate character, racking up more hugs in panel illustrations than any other X-Man in the entirety of the Claremont run, despite leaving the team.

Booy notes, however, that editorial influence (and toy licensing) forced Claremont's hand when Scott's ride into the sunset was undone by editorial mandate in an industry that was just starting to recognize investment in intellectual property (112). Marvel "regarded the character as a corporate asset with value as an active hero" (Booy 113). Nor was this the last time that Claremont's vision for the character would be compromised by commerce. In 1985, Marvel decided to launch a new *X-Men* spinoff without Claremont's cooperation or approval. *X-Factor* (Layton and Guice) would see the four original X-Men (including Cyclops) reunite with Jean Grey, who would be retconned to be still alive, preserved in a cocoon at the bottom of the ocean. As Sean Howe describes it,

> *X-Factor* mangled Claremont's ride-into-the-sunset plans for Scott Summers. . . . instead, Summers deserted his wife and infant son

to be with Jean Grey. Claremont would spend the entire weekend coming up with counterproposals for Monday, but [editor-in-chief] Shooter would shoot them all down. The marketing potential far outweighed Claremont's artistic concerns. (287)

This decision also had a major impact on the symbolic exploration of gender roles that Claremont had built around the character. Abandoning his family to be a superhero again reified the importance of duty and service over the domestic sphere in a way that, instantaneously, reverted Scott to the beginning of his character arc. In a 2020 interview with Astrid Sparks, Claremont said that "it took away the opportunity for Scott to be a father, and it just remade him as tropes" (n.p.).

These tropes can be seen as constituting a sort of tragic repatriation of Scott/Cyclops as a masculine archetype even though, under Claremont, Scott had come to challenge those archetypes and roles to present and personify a masculinity in transition as a direct response to a rise in feminine power.

# CHAPTER 5

# Wolverine as Subversive Masculine Paradigm

The same delicate touch transformed the Wolverine character from a one-note "feisty scrapper" to a layered portrayal of a man torn between nobility and savagery. Claremont gave a soul to his modern samurai, and Wolverine became a breakout hit character.

—GRANT MORRISON, *SUPERGODS*

I t might seem that the easiest subject for exploring masculinity in *X-Men* comics would be Logan/Wolverine. In the eyes of the average comics reader today, Wolverine is a cold-blooded killer, an iconic antihero, and a power fantasy of blood-based hypermasculine problem-solving. Our data does not, however, support this interpretation when it comes to Claremont's Wolverine, who instead demonstrates a complex, dynamic relationship to his own gender identity, one that defines many of the key attributes evinced by the character throughout the run.

Logan/Wolverine's story was largely undefined when Claremont took over the character. At that point, he had appeared in only a handful of comics as an enigmatic Canadian Secret Service operative who joins the X-Men at the behest of Professor X/Charles Xavier. Claremont fleshed out the character quite a bit (with notable help from John Byrne and Barry Windsor-Smith) into a government experiment to create the ultimate killing machine; then, in an exertion of individual agency, Logan decides he does not want to be a killer and abandons his destiny to pursue a so-called higher purpose with the X-Men.

Like Scott/Cyclops, Logan/Wolverine is a white, cisgender male, but not American, at least canonically. His Canadian nationality might have offered an intriguing intersection for the character, but as Vivian Zenari has noted, "the imagined Canada of Wolverine is for the most part the imagining of another country" (58), and though Logan expresses pride in being Canadian,

Wolverine must have national pride, almost out of structural necessity, in order to justify the Canadianness that coalesces around

him. . . . Thus his patriotism might be less than Canadian verisimilitude and more like narrative necessity; or, more like market appeal. (62)

In short, Zenari concludes that Wolverine is identified as Canadian, but
it has little if any impact on the development of his identity, despite stereotypical associations of Canadian nationality with a primitive existence,
something that might be relevant to a character of Wolverine's violent
reputation.

If we look at the numbers, however, we find that Claremont rarely had
Wolverine indulging his baser instincts, and when he does, it is depicted
with grave and lasting consequences. First of all, he is not actually the killing machine that he and others claim him to be, at least not on-panel. In
the entirety of our sample, Wolverine kills four people, the same number as
Havok, which is the second highest. Only Psylocke, as mentioned earlier,
killed more people. Wolverine does instigate fights more than any other
X-Man (and by a wide margin, as seen in figure 5.1), but as the team's chief
brawler and chief spy, that is somewhat expected, especially since he is the
only X-Man to stay on the team for the entirety of the Claremont run.

This dimension is supported through a competing statistic which
shows that as often as Wolverine initiates conflict, he also specifically expresses a reluctance to fight more than any other X-Man, something that
would seem at odds with his violent take-no-prisoners reputation. This
contrast between how our culture views Wolverine and how he was actually developed in the Claremont run may reflect either the general audience's fundamental misunderstanding of Claremont's Logan or a cultural
perception of the character based more on the work of later writers who
themselves may have held (and perpetuated) a fundamental misunderstanding of Claremont's Logan/Wolverine.

This possibility of altering and misunderstanding a character is evident in Charlie Starr's reading of the character. He suggests that when
Claremont left the *X-Men* comics, Wolverine's "animal nature reasserted
itself. Essentially, they started over" (Starr 76). As discussed further
below, this "animal nature" has pivotal connections to Logan's portrayal
of masculinity, and therefore suggests a shift in the cultural perception
of the character that coincided with the revision of Wolverine's character
to one of hegemonic masculinity at the hands of post-Claremont writers. Whereas contemporary depictions of the character frequently present Logan as a sort of simplistic hypermasculine paradigm, Claremont
took a more nuanced approach, allowing Logan to openly interrogate his

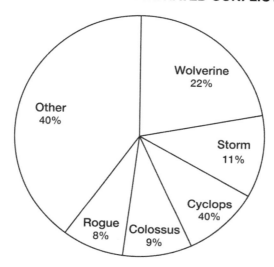

**Fig. 5.1.** *Data ranking of Claremont's* X-Men *characters by how often they instigate conflict.*

relationship to masculinity. Paradoxically, the contrast between Wolverine's surface conformity to hegemonic masculinity in Claremont's run and his ultimate character arc (which often emphasizes the damaging nature of that same masculinity) allows the character to undermine broad masculine gender roles.

As noted by comics scholar Gerri Mahn, Wolverine can represent "the idealized male" (118) in his demonstration of traits such as violence, emotional stoicism, primal virility, and conflicts with other male characters for feminine affection. At the same time, however, all of these masculine traits are portrayed within Claremont's run as innately toxic (though devastatingly effective in many cases) and damaging to Logan/Wolverine's sense of self-worth. Thus, fans of Claremont's Wolverine are able to have it both ways: they can celebrate an icon of idealized masculinity while identifying with a character who openly assesses the cost of those ideals. Because Wolverine is seen as a totem of hegemonic masculinity with cultural capital, it is socially acceptable for people who are themselves performing hegemonic masculinity to celebrate and identify with the character—to buy his comics, wear T-shirts with his likeness, and discuss his most brutal kills with their friends. On the other hand, a huge part of Wolverine's appeal is the kinship that readers feel with a character who struggles to maintain those ideals, and who perceives the extent to which they are destructive. In this, Claremont's Wolverine is a deeply ironic character, one ideally suited for engaging with the subject of toxic masculinity.

This may sound tangential, but one of the real challenges to having open discussions about hegemonic masculinity is the simple fact that engaging in those discussions is considered an unmasculine behavior. It can be a self-sustaining system, and, in this facet, we see the true value of Wolverine within the Claremont run: that he is uniquely embedded within the same cultural paradigms that his author calls into question.

Because Wolverine is a masculine archetype, it is appropriate that the most direct antecedent for a similar performance of masculinity in the early issues of *UXM* is the iconic figure of the cowboy. This connection is most clearly drawn out by Joseph Darowski. In his book *X-Men and the Mutant Metaphor*, he notes that "Logan adopts many of the classic markers of the cowboy. When not in costume, he often wears a cowboy hat and western-themed bolos and belt buckles" (73). And in his essay "When Business Improved Art," Darowski expands the observation:

> Wolverine does take on the role of the outsider on the team, and adopts cowboy imagery, such as a cowboy hat, and mannerisms. The cowboy is an iconic image of a lonesome societal outsider, and traditionally the cowboys in American pop culture are white men who have no racial or gender barrier to acculturation, but nonetheless function outside of society. (42)[1]

Throw in cigars, a checkered and mysterious past, and long wistful stares at dusty horizons, and you have Logan performing to the Marlboro Man stereotype that is so commonly referenced as an emblem of hegemonic masculinity.

As a superhero, Logan is not alone in this capacity to harken back to cowboy mythology. In an essay on the Punisher, Lorrie Palmer identifies how "key aspects of the modern superhero are prefigured in the Western film genre" (281). These aspects are many, but one of the more fundamental of these can be found in "the dialectical relationship between civilization and savagery" (Palmer 284), an iconic theme in the pulp Western tradition, and one that becomes very literal as the dominant internal struggle of Logan/Wolverine, a character who must constantly resist falling into a murderous "berserker rage" in which his animal instincts take over. This is best exemplified in the issue *Wounded Wolf*, which I will conduct a close reading of below.

Outside of the figure of the cowboy, Wolverine's performance of masculinity has also been connected to the same historic politics that inform the figure of the 1970s antihero and its relationship to the concept of masculinity. According to Starr,

> Wolverine's roots may be archetypal, but his cultural beginnings are in the antihero sentiments of the 1970s. We were fresh out of Vietnam, where the presence of news cameras demanded a permanent change in the way wars are waged. In our collective guilt we either condemned war heroes or ignored them, wanting the whole thing to go away. Add to this two factors: First, the more obvious one: the feminist revolution of the sixties and seventies which, while creating opportunities for equality, demonized all things masculine, rejecting such qualities as courage and heroism in favor of sensitivity and emotional expression. The problem with men was that they weren't enough like women. (69)

For Starr, this is what defines Wolverine's relationship to masculinity in the era—a key historical pivot point in Western culture's perception of masculinity, a pivot that Logan was forced to internalize spiritually and externalize by personifying the transition from one era of masculinity to another.

This same connection between epoch and the masculine gender ideal is likewise articulated by Mahn, who also connects it to the elements that inform Wolverine's character.

> The historically accepted narrative of the hegemonic male had been the lynch pin for most gender theories, used to evoke privileged or overtly biased behavior. One of the lasting legacies the three successive waves of feminist movements had was to transform the hegemonic male into an example of oppressive behaviour. (117)

Whereas Starr focuses on Claremont's Wolverine, Mahn focuses on the post-Claremont iteration as it began to deviate from what Claremont had constructed. In Wolverine, we have a hegemonic male superhero who is deeply and consistently traumatized by how perfectly he embodies hegemonic masculinity and the oppressive behaviors that go with it. Instead, he seeks to become more whole (or perhaps simply less miserable) through the recognition and rejection of that masculinity, a process that is all the more difficult because his achievement of the hegemonic ideal has earned him positions of power and agency.

That power and agency make Wolverine valuable—a tactically useful killing machine. Abstractly, this might even align Logan/Wolverine with bell hooks's account of how masculine utility can actually diminish a man's sense of self-worth.

> Caring about men because of what they do for us is not the same as loving males for simply being. When we love maleness, we extend our love whether males are performing or not. Performance is different from simply being. In patriarchal culture males are not allowed simply to be who they are and to glory in their unique identity. Their value is always determined by what they do. In an anti-patriarchal culture males do not have to prove their value and worth. They know from birth that simply being gives them value, the right to be cherished and loved. (*Will to Change* 12)

Thus, Wolverine's performance of masculinity and what it does for the X-Men (ensuring their success, protecting them, and so on) might be seen as an obstacle to his desire to be cherished and loved.

Indeed, over the course of the Claremont run, Logan/Wolverine's masculinity becomes progressively more toxic to his growth as a person and to his overall mental health; in fact, it's killing him. The enemies he has made through his hypermasculine displays come back to haunt him toward the end of the Claremont run, beginning in *Wounded Wolf*. They continue to push him toward a breaking point that Logan only narrowly dodges in the last issues of the series—which he might not have dodged at all had Claremont not been pushed out in the early 1990s. As he explained in interviews, and confirmed in his notebooks (Claremont Papers), Claremont was planning to kill Wolverine outright.[2] Instead, in Claremont's absence, Wolverine would recover and eventually become more powerful than ever before—his healing factor capable of compensating for an escalating series of gruesome (and obviously fatal) injuries.

Interestingly, these superpowers themselves portray fundamental aspects of Wolverine's relationship to masculinity. During his tenure, Claremont frequently integrated the power sets of his characters into the symbolism that they project and speak to. Rogue's powers advance her characterization at a sexual level, whereas Storm's power contributes to her nurturing character, and Kitty's intangibility contributes to her emotional vulnerability, each in compelling ways. Wolverine is no exception, and his superpowers add a great deal to his commentary on masculinity. As Shyminsky notes, "Wolverine's masculinity is dependent on his mutant biology and impossible to achieve outside his fictional realm" ("Mutant Readers" 398). Wolverine's powers all allow him to achieve an extreme masculinity that is not possible in reality.

Wolverine's power set includes unbreakable bones, retractable claws, and a healing factor that repairs injuries at a dramatically accelerated rate. The claws speak, somewhat obviously, to Logan/Wolverine's backstory as a man fighting his own primitive instincts. Visually, they are a sign of open aggression and are frequently displayed to establish that within the narrative. His claws can also be read as phallic in ways that might speak to hypermasculinity once again, with popping claws referring analogously to erections (and thus displays of masculine virility). The fact that these symbolic erections coincide with violent masculine displays (up to and including murder) further reinforces the connection to hypermasculinity.

Wolverine's unbreakable bones provide the type of armored invulnerability that scholar Scott Bukatman identifies as an important part of the superhero fantasy experience, one that is quite specifically linked to masculinity (55). Problematically, however, Bukatman also argues that the mutant body is feminized as a result of the social trauma that it invites from the non-mutants who fear and hate the X-Men. This duality takes perfect shape in the figure of Logan/Wolverine, who is immune to all pain so long as he stays in a primitive berserker state, yet is deeply vulnerable—to pain, shame, guilt, isolation, humiliation—by withholding that primitive drive. As Bukatman notes, the "superhero-fantasy represents an attempt to re-center the self in the body, a reductive conflation of body with subjectivity" (61). This same conflation is central to the cultural practice of gender essentialism, however, and Wolverine's desire to define himself beyond a body built for violence therefore provides an intriguing perspective on the subject of bodily essentialism.

The character's healing factor is more complex. On the one hand, the ability to recover quickly from injury contributes to the same sort of armored fantasy that Bukatman speaks to, but it also allows for a somewhat contradictory portrayal of pain and suffering. Because he can heal, Wolverine can be shown to endure increasingly horrific injuries, thus creating the opportunity for a visual spectacle that amounts to body horror—a spectacle of flowing blood and shredded flesh that visually reads as masculine suffering, while at the same time the narrative context assures us that he will be fine, that his suffering is temporary. In this, Wolverine's powers can make him into a performance of masculine ritual, allowing him to present the grimmest wounds but always coming back, rarely showing any pain, and rarely suffering any long-term consequences.

**Fig. 5.2.** *Jubilee removes a spear from Wolverine's body in* The Path Not Taken! (UXM, *vol. 1, no. 275). Jim Lee, penciler.*

We can see Claremont playing with Logan's performance of masculinity quite actively in a number of stories. *Wounded Wolf*, discussed below, is a great example, but so too is *Fever Dream* (*UXM* no. 251), in which Wolverine is crucified and tortured by the cyborg Donald Pierce, or the scene from *The Path Not Taken!* (*UXM* no. 275) in which Wolverine forces Jubilee to pull a spear out of him so he can pursue a supervillain (fig. 5.2). In all cases, Claremont frames the scenes from the viewpoint of an innocent (and female) character who is horrified by Wolverine's suffering. While we might argue that this creates a gendered contrast to enhance Wolverine's hypermasculine displays, it is important to note that the viewpoint character is also a reader stand-in, and thus the audience shares the female character's sense of horror.

As a side note, it is important to remember that Wolverine's healing factor has established limits within the Claremont run, whereas later authors would take situations to extremes in order to ramp up the character's hypermasculine aspects. In contrast, Claremont's main arc with Wolverine in the final years of his run revolves around the character's diminishment as his healing factor begins to falter and the years of wear and tear start to overwhelm him, leaving him a shadow of his former self. In this light, Claremont's Wolverine becomes increasingly vulnerable as he becomes increasingly human. Post-Claremont, Wolverine's healing power becomes, essentially, a form of immortality, with no explanation given for the so-called power creep.

Although Wolverine's immortality was developed after the Claremont run, we can also move backward to build further context for Wolverine's performance of gender in the broader *X-Men* universe. Here, again, the data from our project is relevant. As noted earlier, only 4 out of the 66 issues of pre-Claremont *X-Men* comics passed the Bechdel test, while in the first 500 issues of *UXM*, spanning 1963–2008, the issues outside of Claremont's run passed the Bechdel test a pitiful 33 percent of the time, compared to 82 percent during Claremont's tenure. Although the quantitative data is compelling, the qualitative data (interpreting the story mechanics) lines up with it perfectly.

When Claremont inherited *X-Men*, the characters were predominantly male and frequently engaged in aggressive internal bickering accompanied by aggressive masculine posturing. This is a tradition that, in some ways, traces back through *X-Men* history to the innately misogynistic struggle for the affections of Jean Grey on the part of the four other X-Men, as discussed in the previous chapter. This competition extended to Professor X himself, who also claims he is in love with Jean.

This overall dynamic is established in the very first issue of *X-Men*, with the male characters pitting themselves against each other in pursuit of Jean's affections. In *X-Men* (*UXM* no. 1), Professor X introduces the X-Men to Jean by stating, "You may be interested to learn that at this very moment I sense a taxi approaching our main gate! Within that vehicle is a new pupil. A most attractive young lady" (7). Three of the four male X-Men then immediately, despite never having met her, express adoration for Jean as they gaze out the window, before fawning over her, flirting with her, and even (in one case) grabbing and trying to kiss her (8–10). This is all within their first moments of meeting Jean, and it establishes a trend of internal competition based around the sort of archetypal masculine rituals frequently found in popular culture narratives of the 1960s. Simply put, women were trophies to be won by men through competition.

Claremont's work initially pursued a similar dynamic, with Wolverine and Cyclops competing for Jean's affection while Colossus, Banshee, and Nightcrawler compete for Storm's. As will be discussed below, the latter romantic conflict is quite brief and recontextualized as a platonic bond once Claremont gets firmer footing. The Wolverine versus Cyclops conflict runs a little longer but likewise finds resolution in the first few years of the Claremont run. Though iconic, the Cyclops/Jean/Wolverine love triangle is pretty much resolved by *UXM* no. 118, titled *The Submergence of Japan*, when Wolverine meets Mariko, his other famously doomed love interest.

That particular scene is loaded with the trappings of gender commentary. Wolverine is frustrated (as is often the case), wandering alone to a traditional Japanese garden in search of solitude. He reflects, "Man I should'a stayed in the Savage Land. I got no use for civilization. Too many rules. Too many flamin' people sayin' NO! I want to cut loose every time I fight but I gotta hold back." Suddenly, he realizes that he is not alone in the beautiful, intricately coordinated garden. Mariko Yashida is there. He then becomes self-conscious of his violent appearance and thinks to himself that he has to be careful not to "spook her." They talk, express admiration for each other, and he even starts to tell her his real name (a significant admission as this had not yet been revealed to any of his teammates) before being interrupted by an earthquake. That necessitates that he pop his claws to become a hero again, thus interrupting the moment through the combination of the call to heroism and the hypermasculine attributes by which Wolverine achieves it. Predictably, Mariko is frightened (*The Submergence of Japan* 16–18).

Thus, by juxtaposing Logan's savagery to both the lovely garden and the beautiful woman he meets there, Claremont portrays Wolverine's hypermasculine attributes as antithetical to his desires. He also takes Logan outside of the traditional love triangle narrative that so frequently manifests in superhero comics of the era. Wolverine never stops having feelings for Jean, but he respects her agency in choosing Cyclops over him. The contest is over, and instead of hypermasculine displays, Logan's pursuit of Mariko will be based on mutual respect, civility, honor, and loyalty. Although this is largely oriented around the potentially sexist samurai mythology (discussed below), Claremont's cultivation of Mariko's character and agency helps to alleviate that transference.

In this reshuffling of character romance dynamics, Claremont achieves escape velocity from the initial, highly sexist mechanics of the earliest *X-Men* issues. It has to be noted, however, that Claremont's vision of Wolverine also had to evolve from the portrayal of the character by his creator Len Wein, who wrote Logan as a guest character in *The Incredible Hulk* nos. 180–181 (Wein and Trimpe), and then again in *Giant-Size X-Men* no. 1 (Wein and Cockrum). In the latter appearance, Logan/Wolverine's introduction to *X-Men* readers again conforms entirely to hegemonic masculinity as Logan breaks up a meeting of military officials with an aggressively hypermasculine display: "Let them wait. It's good for the soul. All right, gents—I'm here! Now who's the bigwig you want me to meet?" He then proceeds to insult a man in a wheelchair and renege on his agreement with the Canadian military before threatening his boss with a razor-sharp claw and challenging the man to come after him as he leaves—all in a two-page intro (Wein and Cockrum 5–6). As R. W. Connell notes, men's use of violence is an important facet of gender power (Introduction xx). As such, Wolverine's initial depiction as a symbol of violence aligns him with that important aspect of hegemonic masculinity. This resurfaces later in the issue when he chastises his teammates for retreating: "You lilay-livers want to scatter, that's swell but the Wolverine is going out for blood!" (Wein and Cockrum 40). In both scenes, and others, Wein's portrayal of Wolverine is unironically hypermasculine, thus establishing a starting point on the far extreme of the masculine spectrum from which Claremont would move his character in order to get Wolverine to the subversive portrayal of masculinity that Claremont eventually constructs.

One of the early elements that Claremont used to first communicate Logan/Wolverine's resistance to hegemonic masculinity is Logan's underlying sensitivity. Though characterized as savage and asocial in some iterations, Claremont's Wolverine consistently demonstrates an emotional intelligence and sense of empathy beyond that of any other X-Man (with the possible exception of Nightcrawler, his best friend). In this manner, he is exhibiting a nurturing capability that is very much associated with femininity at this point in comics history, one that would seem to be at odds with the violent and primitive portrayal of masculinity that he otherwise exhibited simultaneously.

We are introduced to this paradox very early on in the Claremont run when Storm hurts Logan/Wolverine's feelings by portraying him as a cold-blooded hunter. In *UXM* no. 109, titled *Home Are the Heroes!*, Logan mentions he wants to go hunting. Storm becomes upset with this, asking, "You would take the lives of innocent animals—not for survival but merely for sport?!" Logan quickly seizes the moral authority, however, by responding, "I said huntin', honeybunch—I said nothin' about killin'. It takes no skill t'kill. What takes skill is sneakin' up close enough to a skittish doe t'touch her." Storm immediately apologizes for misjudging him (thus functioning as a reader surrogate in this scene). Logan replies, "You've all been misjudgin' me since the day I joined this turkey outfit" (15).

Not long after, in *To Save the Savage Land* (*UXM* no. 116), Banshee says of Storm (a character he has recently expressed physical attraction toward), "I'd better see if she's all right," after a harrowing incident in which she tried, and failed, to save a villain from falling into a chasm. But Wolverine puts a hand on his shoulder and tells him to leave her be. "Think about it. She went down that hole to save a life. She came up empty-handed. Whatever happened down there, I figure it's somethin' she'd rather work out on her own" (30). In this scene, Wolverine expresses empathy and understanding for Storm (in sharp contrast to Banshee's potentially lascivious faux-sympathy). From there, multiple scenes in the series continue to showcase Wolverine's enhanced sense of empathy, including understanding Colossus's need for motivation (*UXM* no. 122) and Kitty's need to be taken seriously (*UXM* no. 168).

Logan shows further emotional empathy through mentoring various junior X-Men. Although he openly rejects the leadership role that Professor X had been grooming him for, he nonetheless becomes a highly effective mentor. At various points he can be seen to mentor Kurt, Peter, Kitty, Alex, Alison, Jubilee, and the entire Power Pack (a group of child superheroes)—to name just a few—in each case showing his character's nurturing side. This push toward nurturing is emblematic of one of the more fundamental relationships of the Claremont run: the one between Storm and Wolverine. At first the characters appear to be two extremes of gender identity, but they progressively adopt aspects of each other's gender performance while playing off of each other in important and definitive ways. Ramzi Fawaz suggests that one of the appeals of the X-Women may be "witnessing female characters inhabit classically masculine forms of power," which he describes as "a deviant form of female masculinity" (215). We could argue the same effect in seeing Wolverine inhabit classically masculine forms of power. Broadly speaking, the contrast between Wolverine and Storm (as discussed in depth earlier) allows each of them to help the other transgress their respective gender roles. For example, Claremont may use the hypermasculine Wolverine to validate Storm's position as leader, but he might also use her femininity to empower and validate his subservient position within the hierarchy.

Indeed, Miles Booy argues that in early portrayals Wolverine is symbolic of a primitive masculinity (through "ferocity"), whereas Storm symbolizes, in contrast, "feminine grace" through her primitive closeness to nature (26). They are presented as idealized visions of naturalized and essentialized (through primitivity) gender paradigms (earth goddess and savage beast, respectively). This coincides with Gerri Mahn's reading of Wolverine, in which the "more bestial he became the more unbound and pronounced his manhood" (119). It is all the more important, therefore, to see Wolverine and Storm progressively deviate from those paradigms in tandem and in a collaborative manner.

According to Carol Cooper, the portrayal of female characters in positions of power in *UXM* has a ripple effect on the male characters, allowing them to exhibit traits that were traditionally associated with feminine gender roles. "One unexpected side benefit of showing females as leaders is how their less impassive demeanour makes it okay for men to show emotional warmth, doubt, vulnerability and other qualities that might otherwise be considered unproductively effeminate" (Cooper 197). As described in the previous chapter, we see such a relationship take shape between Cyclops and Phoenix, but we can also see it quite clearly in Wolverine's relationship to Storm, thus creating a parallel codependence in their respective gender performances. Because this relationship was discussed already in a previous chapter, I would simply reiterate here that there seems to be a complex, gender-queering aspect inherent in Storm and Wolverine's relationship.

Moving beyond the bigger, abstract aspects of Wolverine's masculinity, we can isolate the progression of his gender portrayal through close readings of a series of touchstone issues for the character in general (not just in terms of his relationship to gender). That these two elements (character and gender portrayal) intersect so perfectly is by no means a coincidence. Arguably, the two most definitive Wolverine stories are *Wolverine: Alone!* (*UXM* no. 133, part of the *Dark Phoenix Saga*) and *Wounded Wolf* (*UXM* no. 205). As benchmarks in both the character's evolution and progression (one for establishing his potential as a violent solo character, and one for establishing his internal conflict with violence) they merit closer analysis.

*Wolverine: Alone!* is widely regarded as the point in comics continuity where the character emerged as a popular and dynamic superhero. The setup is simple: the rest of the X-Men have been captured by the Hellfire Club, while Wolverine (alone) is left for dead in the sewers. What follows is a heroic tale that can be seen as a mix of *Die Hard* with Dickens as Wolverine fights his way upward through Claremont's spatial-metaphor setting. Each subsequent level of the Hellfire Club represents a tier of society that Wolverine has to fight through, with the inner circle of the Hellfire Club at the top, in the library. This metaphor intersects class (in particular, a North American perspective on class) and masculinity in some interesting ways.

In the basement of the Hellfire Club, Wolverine encounters the club's security forces and ambushes them aggressively. He quickly dispatches them but finds himself cornered by the final guard, who has him in his gunsights. Unphased, Wolverine taunts him:

> Hey, Bub, I know what you're thinkin'. "He's hurt, an' he's five me-
> ters away from me, an' I got a full clip of ammo in my rifle. Ques-
> tion is: can I kill Wolverine before he can reach me an' cut me into
> shish-kebab with those freaky claws of his?" Well, bub, Wolverine is
> virtually unkillable. Wolverine's claws are adamantium, the strongest
> metal known—capable of slicin' through vanadium steel like a hot
> knife through butter. An' five meters o' floor aint much distance—fer
> me. It's your play, hero. I'm waitin'. (*Wolverine: Alone!* 6)

As the mercenary drops his rifle in surrender, Wolverine laments, "Shoot, I was hopin' you'd go for it." The scene presents a direct homage to the fa-mous "Do you feel lucky, punk?" scene from 1971's *Dirty Harry*, in which rogue police detective Dirty Harry Callahan, played by masculine icon Clint Eastwood, says to a criminal,

> I know what you're thinking: "Did he fire six shots or only five?"
> Well, to tell you the truth, in all this excitement, I've kinda lost track
> myself. But being this is a .44 Magnum, the most powerful handgun
> in the world, and would blow your head clean off, you've got to ask
> yourself one question: "Do I feel lucky?" Well, do you, punk?

Both as a test of violent courage in the face of mortal danger, and by al-lusion to an iconic hypermasculine film portrayal of an antihero, the se-quence aligns Wolverine directly with hegemonic masculinity. All of this is to say that if *Wolverine: Alone!* is indeed the moment when Logan/Wol-verine emerges as an important and relatable character, he does so while performing hegemonic masculinity to the utmost. Although that contra-dicts some of the earlier gender-queer elements described above, it does enhance Wolverine's subversive potential by establishing his ethos as a popular masculine paradigm.

Adding a significant intersection of class to the primitive component of Wolverine's hypermasculine display is the contrasting antagonists, cre-ated in part by the Victorian-era aesthetic embraced by the Hellfire Club. Wolverine is not just attacking rich people (and, more problematically, their servants), he is punching out people in powdered wigs and silken cravats, thus potentially connoting an assault on British imperialism or class privilege itself, both of which represent longstanding enemies of masculinity in American popular culture at large. For example, anthropologist E. B. Tylor famously wrote in his 1871 treatise *Primitive Culture* that the progress of civilization is the "onward movement from barbarism" (23), but also (in consequence) an affront to masculinity, something Tylor valued greatly. Picking up that thread, Bradley Deane, in his 2008 article "Imperial Barbarians: Primitive Masculinity in Lost World Fiction," suggests that the progression from barbarism to civility did indeed undermine masculine culture in complex (perhaps even contradictory) ways in Victorian adventure serials such as the Allan Quatermain stories of H. Rider Haggard and David Maule (205).

Wolverine's emergence as a hero is thus deeply entangled (intentionally and unintentionally) with a wide variety of signifiers of another wide variety of complex masculinities. The fact that he is described by Claremont as "having the time of his life" (2) in this issue suggests a naturalness to his hypermasculine violence. As Wolverine makes his way through the Hellfire Club one tier at a time, encountering goons in the basement, the rich and powerful on the main floor, then the Illuminati-like Hellfire Club members upstairs, he fights his way to the upper echelons of a corrupt and brutal world that is hiding behind the mask of civility. His ability to punch (or stab) his way to resolution again aggrandizes violence as a masculine problem-solving skill in a manner that is deeply reminiscent of the complex conflicts between masculine heroes and so-called feminized civilizations that we see in the pulp-era adventure serials that Deane describes.

Also, it is worth noting that once Wolverine reaches the inner circle of the Hellfire Club, three members are literally knocked down a tier in the fight, two of them straight into the underground, and one through a railing to the main floor, thus fulfilling the promise that the spatial metaphor of the issue sets up. Metaphorically, Wolverine has dismantled the hierarchy and primitivized the elite, forcing them to battle for their lives in the underground, just as he did at the start of the story. It is therefore safe to say that Wolverine rides a wave of violent masculinity to his initial position of prominence within the cultural zeitgeist. After penciler/co-plotter John Byrne's departure from the book as of *UXM* no. 144, Claremont continued to cultivate a more nuanced portrayal of Wolverine, one that positions his violent masculinity as antithetical to the character's higher-level being, thus creating a classic Apollonian/Dionysian divide.

According to Friedrich Nietzsche's theory of Apollonian and Dionysian values (articulated in *The Birth of Tragedy* [1872]), all beings experience an internal conflict that is both universal and innately dramatic—thus, in Nietzsche's eyes, ideal for cultural representation. Apollo is the Greek god of enlightenment, and Dionysus the god of alcohol, orgies, and actual berserker rages, highly similar to those that Wolverine falls into. For Nietzsche, what made Greek tragedy the pinnacle of theater was the Greeks' unique ability to portray the fundamental conflict of these two gods within the spirit of literally every human being: we all constantly pose our rational selves against our primal desires. As such, Nietzsche believed that Greek tragedy was more fundamentally human and relatable (even subconsciously) than anything Western society had written since, better even than Shakespeare. If Wolverine is successful in embodying this conflict (to any degree), then Nietzsche's theory (paired with Claremont's ideal for the character) speaks to Logan/Wolverine's appeal—not as a scrappy guy with sharp claws, but as a dynamic personification of a universal human struggle, one that, again, is deeply connected to gender identity.

We see this quite directly in Claremont's notebooks (Claremont Papers). His original vision for the Wolverine miniseries is first expressed in the relationship between Mariko and Yukio as reflective of Logan/Wolverine's personal journey. He outlines it as shown in figure 5.3. The Apollonian/Dionysian divide is evident here, but so too is the more controversial decision to personify Logan's choice within that divide in the form of a pair of female love interests. Again we see gender defining the character.

The four-issue Wolverine miniseries of 1982, penciled by Frank Miller, has been identified by scholar Eric Sobel as being among "the first superhero comics to extensively represent Japanese culture from an American perspective" (226). The story integrates samurai/bushido mythology into the Wolverine backstory and culminates with his engagement to Mariko Yashida, thus reflecting a clear winner in terms of the Apollonian/Dionysian conflict. Logan/Wolverine chooses duty and honor, and to be a man instead of an animal.[3]

At the same time, of course, Wolverine's performance of hegemonic masculinity reflects yet another hypermasculine archetype in the form of the ronin (the master-less samurai). As Annette Schad-Seifert notes in her analysis of masculinity in samurai mythology, the samurai (like the cowboy archetype discussed earlier) is largely a cultural invention reflecting a society's need to grieve older masculinities in the face of a civilizing world that has no place for the old guard (205). Where the figure of the ronin offers new ground for Logan/Wolverine, however, is in the incorporation of duty, honor, loyalty, and obligation—all major themes of this particular narrative arc. As such, the story allows him to evolve progressively. By aligning the character with the ronin rather than the cowboy, Claremont

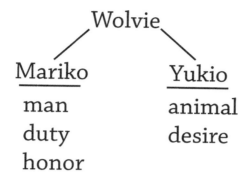

**Fig. 5.3.** *A re-creation of Claremont's notebook entry on the Wolverine miniseries (Claremont Papers).*

simply slides Logan/Wolverine toward a masculine archetype that offers him more opportunity to explore effeminate characteristics in the eyes of a Western audience. This establishes a trajectory for the character's relationship to gender that would be continued over the course of many years to come, taking him further along and eventually outside the bushido mythology altogether.

Again, however, we have another social category intersecting with Wolverine's gender performance. As Sobel notes,

> In *Wolverine*, Claremont and Miller revel in "Japanese" stereotypes, both in terms of imagery but more importantly in their representation of the values that supposedly contribute to Japanese identity. Wolverine's love interest in the miniseries, Mariko, and her father, Shingen, are exemplary of the stifling strictures that Orientalizing brings to Japanese characters in the large mediascape of American superhero comics. (226–227)

The stereotypes that Sobel identifies include an exaggerated portrayal of gender division in Japanese society, one in which female characters such as the androgynous ronin Yukio can only exhibit deviance from archaic feminine gender roles by operating outside of social expectations altogether, and the hyperfeminine Mariko—whom Sobel connects to the trope of "The Geisha and the White Man" (229)—becomes a trophy to be won through a violent duel. Thus a particular brand of Japanese femininity that proliferated in popular culture (particularly in North America) is used to define the white masculinity of Logan through, as Sobel argues, appropriative means. Needless to say, this is a complex negotiation of identity across lines of gender, class, and transnational cultures.

Nonetheless, we can also see the shift from cowboy to samurai holding sway in our data set. In the first 75 *UXM* issues in which he appeared (all of which preceded the miniseries), Wolverine instigates 22 fights, for an average of 0.29 instigations per issue. In his next 107 issues in the Claremont run (all of which take place after the miniseries), that number drops to 0.21 instigations per issue, despite the character's surging popularity and increased position of prominence (including a number of solo stories). Although an 8 percent drop in the number of instigations might seem insignificant, within a contextualized mixed-methods approach it is actually quite telling. As Logan/Wolverine became more prominent, he picked fewer fights.

After the Logan/Wolverine miniseries and the cultivation of his relationship to bushido culture, the next major milestone issue for the character was *Wounded Wolf* (*UXM* no. 205). Wolverine is the only X-Man to appear in the issue. In the entire Claremont run, only seven issues feature just a single X-Man throughout the entire issue, and *Wounded Wolf* is Claremont's only solo Wolverine story.

The story opens with a body-horror prologue in which much-admired guest artist Barry Windsor-Smith showcases the horrific transformation of the issue's antagonist.[4] Oyama Yuriko (aka Lady Deathstrike) undergoes a grotesque procedure that transforms her from a human into a cyborg.[5] Yuriko had recently been defeated by Wolverine and Alpha Flight in *Alpha Flight* nos. 33–34 (Mantlo) after she sought to reclaim Wolverine's adamantium skeleton, which she sees as the intellectual property of her deceased father. After that failure, she makes a deal with the villainous magic-user Spiral to grant her the power to destroy Logan/Wolverine.

The first thing to note here is that Claremont provides Wolverine with an antagonist who is a woman in command of three inferior cyborgs (who, it is later revealed, are the victims of Wolverine's rampage from *Wolverine: Alone!*). In appropriate masculine fashion, they too have a score to settle with Wolverine, identifying him as "the man we hate most in the world" (*Wounded Wolf* 3). Their hatred of Wolverine reflects the endless cycle of violence that is so foundational to discussions of justice and the need for civilized systems of retribution, as we see in the *Oresteia* of Aeschylus, which famously chronicles the establishment of the Athenian justice system as an alternative to primitive revenge. *Wounded Wolf* offers a parallel track to Aeschylus's most famous trilogy, ultimately suggesting a better way through nonviolence.

After the prologue, the battle begins *in medias res*, with five-year-old Power Pack heroine Katie Power encountering a brutally wounded Wolverine on the streets of New York after her caretaker is knocked unconscious by his pursuers (Lady Deathstrike and her cyborg squad). The cyborg Cole runs past Katie, gun blazing, as he says, "Man, who'da figured that crazy mutie could even move after what Deathstrike did to him" (5). Instinctively, Wolverine grabs Katie to take her out of harm's way, but she is scared of him (despite knowing him from previous issues) due to his feral, mute state.

In *Wounded Wolf*, Katie's innate fear of Wolverine's primal ferocity can be productively viewed as a metaphor for his relationship to masculinity and his journey from animal to person. As Connell notes, "Men are substantially excluded from relationships with very young children" (247), which is in keeping with the delineation of nurturing as feminine and the absence thereof as masculine. Over the course of the issue, Logan/Wolverine regains his senses, and, in doing so, he also regains Katie's trust and friendship, which Logan considers deeply valuable assets.

Windsor-Smith drew Wolverine with the familiar black lines of blood that were a mainstay during the Comics Code Authority era. Although the ink lines are hard to identify as streams of blood, Wolverine is bleeding profusely. His clothes have disintegrated with the exception of his left boot, his exterior briefs, and his belt. The near nudity serves as a display of primal masculinity, much in keeping with Booy's reading on shows of flesh for Wolverine in general. Booy goes so far as to suggest that stripping Wolverine of his clothes symbolizes stripping him of his humanity (31). This is certainly a fair interpretation here, if not in other instances where nudity can reflect things such as vulnerability, comfort, intimacy, and so on. Wolverine, in this instance, may be as far from human as readers have ever seen him, and Katie, as a stand-in for the audience, is given a glimpse into his repressed bestial nature—the animal within—and she is terrified.

The near-nudity also enhances the sense of vulnerability through both the exposed flesh and the contrasting blizzard that Claremont weaves into the story, and which Windsor-Smith ably articulates in every panel with gusts of ice, falling snow, and a blood-spattered base of snow on the ground. Again, Wolverine is exposed, this time to the elements, in a way that establishes a sort of pathetic fallacy in which nature is just as assailing, chaotic, and dominant as the cyborgs pursuing him.

**Fig. 5.4.** *Wolverine in* Wounded Wolf *(UXM, vol. 1, no. 205). Barry Windsor-Smith, penciler.*

Together, Wolverine and Katie try to escape in a taxi, but it too is attacked by the cyborg assault team. Wolverine throws Katie and the driver clear before the taxi is destroyed, but he is caught in the explosion. As he emerges from the wreck, his back aflame, the narrator tells us, "Her first—and only—reaction is to cry. Tears come unbidden—flow unstopped—rough surrogates for emotions too great for voice or gesture" (11). Here we see a clear example of the feminized viewpoint character and its capacity to configure the spectacle of Wolverine's bodily suffering as horrific rather than glorious.

As Logan/Wolverine starts to regain himself, his first words to Katie are in Japanese: "Boku wa dare?"—"Who am I?" Then he speaks again: <"What am I?">—also in Japanese (as indicated by the < > marks), but this time translated into English for the reader. He then lets out a bestial "Rahrrr" that further horrifies the little girl: "Again, Katie's eyes burn with tears. Not, this time for the pain of his body, but for the terrible anguish of his voice" (12). He then regains his ability to speak English, telling her (and us) that "the same way my healing factor repairs my body, it's restorin' my mind" (13). Katie offers to help by using lethal force against their pursuers, but Logan, now in his right mind and faculties, refuses to let her.

> "You will not."
> "But they're trying to kill you!"
> "That's my look-out."
> "I want to help!"
> "You've done so—buyin' time for me to heal. These are old friends of mine, Katie, with old scores to settle. This is a grudge fight. Leave them to me."
> "But what'll I do?!"
> "Maybe the hardest thing you've ever done, an' the bravest. I want you to trust me." (*Wounded Wolf* 14)

On the one hand, this could easily be interpreted as the typical male hero sidelining the female hero through an act of condescending chivalry. On the other hand, however, the scene evinces the great value of civility and the inherent negatives of the endless cycle of violence (a cycle that Deathstrike, as antagonist, is clearly both the victim and perpetrator of). In keeping the next generation from that cycle, and by taking the time to explain this to a five-year-old girl while identifying the courage of her innocence, Wolverine is expressing a more fundamental aspect of his own character and of the choices he has made. This is his fight, but he is not reveling in it. It is nothing more than his past catching up with him, and he will not allow Katie (whom he speaks to like an equal) to fall into the same trap.

Claremont then shifts to Deathstrike's perspective, which reinforces Katie's capacity to influence Logan/Wolverine in a way that makes him less dangerous. She informs her comrades, "The girl makes Wolverine vulnerable. Find her—take her hostage—and our battle is won" (15). But here, Claremont constructs a complex moral consideration that is directly the opposite of Deathstrike's presumption that empathy, compassion, and even vulnerability are exclusively weaknesses. Katie is not endangering Wolverine—she's saving him.

As detailed in *Alpha Flight* no. 33 (Mantlo), the first appearance of Yuriko as Lady Deathstrike, it was Heather MacDonald's nurturing that brought Logan/Wolverine back from his initial feral state after he was experimented on by the government, and it was Logan's love for Heather that motivated him to leave Canada to join the X-Men, where his love of Jean Grey further integrated him into his found family, as did the platonic love he later felt for Storm and then Kitty. Wolverine's story is consistently about a hypermasculine creation finding himself through encounters with feminine nurturer figures. Thus, the debt that Wolverine feels toward such figures might explain his appreciation for traditionally feminine-nurturer characteristics, or even a desire to cultivate his own nurturing side, despite living in a society that insists he perform a gender identity that sees such cultivation as a threat to the binary.

I would even go so far as to argue that this juxtaposition of gender identity (polarized into who he is versus what he needs) is perhaps one of the more compelling and intriguing aspects of Wolverine as a character, and a major source of his subconscious appeal to generations of readers. In *Wounded Wolf*, Katie Power is the stand-in for that tradition. In that sense, it is significant that his momentary ward in this issue be feminine (as most of Wolverine's young students are). As with the Mariko/Yukio divide described earlier, Wolverine must again choose which aspect of himself to follow by choosing to conform with either the way of Katie (innocence and compassion) or of Lady Deathstrike (a life of violent posturing and conflict).

Deathstrike, it must be noted, is acting to avenge her father and brother. Her motivation is patrilineal, and thus she seeks to restore the honor of her family through masculinized means. Her transformation in the body shop may be symbolic of her need to transcend the sexual assignment of her body and become an androgynous creature instead. She still manifests feminine characteristics, however—through her name, Lady Deathstrike; through her enormously long fingernails, which are her main weapon; and through a costume that exposes her cleavage. In this sense, Deathstrike is herself a gender-queer character, ideally suited (again) to the lens of Donna Harraway's theory of cyborg feminism. We might even say the same of Katie, to some degree, a little girl in pigtails who is also a powerhouse superhero.

As Wolverine violently shreds the body of Deathstrike, making the cybernetic elements more and more apparent, he is shocked at what he sees.

> "My God. Yuriko?!!"
> "It . . . was necessary . . . to become like you."
> "The better to slay me? My healing factor makes me a mutant, lacing my bones with adamantium an' giving me these claws—that was done *to* me. But—you asked to be changed. You did this to yourself. Threw away a humanity I'd give pretty near anything to possess." (20)

Yuriko responds by begging Wolverine to kill her. Again, his reaction reveals his perspective on himself:

> "That'd solve all your problems wouldn't it? But it won't be that easy. You made me an animal again, Deathstrike—took me back to a time in my life . . . I thought I'd put behind me. Animal and man, each has his reasons for killing. None apply here."
> "Show mercy, I beg you. Let me free!"

Wolverine, sheathing his claws (an important symbolic gesture given their phallic symbolism), simply responds, "earn it" (20–21).

In this scene, Wolverine shows his ultimate disdain for Deathstrike's choices, and his own ultimate desire. He is repulsed by her ambition to be like him when he wants nothing more than to be someone else. Through cybernetic enhancement, Deathstrike had become a violent and powerful creature, able to inflict her will upon others while she is rendered more androgynous by the aesthetic surrounding her. In that capacity, she seeks to drag Wolverine back toward his own animal nature, one associated quite clearly with stereotypes of masculinity (if not toxic masculinity, in particular).

On the final page of *Wounded Wolf*, Wolverine walks over to where Katie is hiding. When she asks what he did, he says,

> "I won't lie, Katie-girl. There's a part of me as wild an' fierce as my name-sake. I'm a hard man—given to hard ways. When I fight, it's to win. That isn't pretty, an it sure isn't nice. But bein' a man—that means choosin' to grow an' change an' put aside the old ways. Some people can't—or worse, won't—do that."
> "Like that lady an' her creeps?"
> "Yup."

"That's sad."

"Yup."

"I was scared of you, Mr. Wolverine."

"I know. Are you still?"

"A little."

"No matter what happens—ever—you'll always have a friend to run to, Katie. That is, if you want?"

"An' so, Mr. Logan, will you."

"C'mon darling—storm's liftin'—Let's go home." (22)

And thus the issue ends with a scared little girl grabbing Wolverine's blood-drenched hand (now an instrument of affection rather than aggression), and they walk off together.

In the dialogue quoted here, Katie establishes what might be her entire purpose in this story: to ensure that the issue's violence is interpreted as brutal and traumatizing rather than balletic and beautiful, as comic book violence can sometimes be rendered. Interpreted in that pro-violence light, this would be a story about Wolverine being awesome, rather than a complex commentary on the historical cycle of violence and the ways that the association of violence with hegemonic masculinity can hamper an individual's development as a person. Wolverine's specific expression of a need to let the old ways go, in light of all the intersecting symbols of gender performance, might encapsulate the gender-queer elements of the story as well.

If we want a traditional literary comparison, Katie's expression of fear in encountering her friend Logan/Wolverine is nicely reminiscent of the famous scene from Homer's *Iliad* where the young Astyanax sees his father, Hector, in his full armor and weeps in fear:

> This said, he reacht to take his sonne, who (of his armes afraid,
> And then the horse-haire plume, with which he was so overlaid
> Nodded so horribly), he clingd back to his nurse and cride.
> (bk. 6, 506–508)

As with the comparison to Aeschylus, what we see here is a complex commentary on the cycle of violence. In both instances, the message is clear that Wolverine's pursuit of pacifism is difficult. As Booy notes, "The narrative compromise would often be stories where the X-Men were so completely beaten and imprisoned by powerful foes that only the eruption of Logan's innate nature could save them—his violence was thus rendered as an unfortunate narrative necessity" (31). If you push him, he will regress. The inclusion of Katie Power in *Wounded Wolf* speaks to this very directly by creating the perfect foil for Wolverine, providing both an incentive to persist, and a contrast to reflect how far he's fallen. Without her presence, the entire story becomes an aristeia—a glorious celebration of Wolverine finally cutting loose.[6] With her, it can be more than that.

We see this exact strategy extended to the broader character arc. Even beyond the Claremont run, Wolverine is repeatedly paired up with innocent young female protégés, thus giving him the opportunity to cultivate the gender-queer nurturing element that was fundamental to his initial transformation from beast to person. In this regard, Claremont might characterize isolation as bestial and community as civil. This theme will be revisited on multiple occasions through Wolverine's character. When left on his own, he regresses. When integrated into a supportive and loving community such as the X-Men, he progressively improves in his quest to evolve beyond his primitive berserker state.

The fact that this quest is ultimately Wolverine's arc is what allows the character to deviate from the older masculine archetypes that he draws from. Whereas the American cowboy or the Japanese ronin or even Dirty Harry himself all signal a nostalgic lament for a traditional, or even primitive, form of masculinity, Claremont's Wolverine, a character who has himself achieved a level of cultural capital that is in many ways on par with these other archetypes, is allowed to evolve.

# CHAPTER 6

# A Spectrum of "Men"

## *Refracting Masculinities through Nightcrawler and Havok*

> The original concept of Nightcrawler was that he was an angry, bitter, tormented soul. You know, "I'm trapped in the body of a monster." Well, Dave [Cockrum] and I both felt we'd seen that movie before. It's exactly what a reader would expect seeing someone who is blue and furry, has two toes, three fingers, fangs and a tail. But what if he wasn't? . . . And once you cross that line and say, "It's not my problem. It's how you choose to look at me, not how I am. This is who I am. Accept it or not, but it's not my fault." That gives you, as a writer, a tremendous amount of freedom to comment on how people perceive other people.
>
> –CHRIS CLAREMONT, QUOTED IN JOSEPH J. DAROWSKI, *X-MEN AND THE MUTANT METAPHOR*

As with the feminine cosmology of *Uncanny X-Men* (*UXM*), Claremont's *X-Men* issues also feature a broad spectrum of male-performing characters. Each one has a complex relationship to gender performance that is further complicated by their character's relationships with others, such as Wolverine and Cyclops, who embody and project traditional masculine archetypes with the potential to progressively undermine them. In this sense, characters like Nightcrawler and Havok (who is Cyclops's brother) offer the potential to refract the masculine gender role of Wolverine and Cyclops discussed in earlier chapters. Where Wolverine and Cyclops achieve (but do not embrace) the role of the alpha male by the standards of Bronze Age (1970–1985) Marvel comics, both Nightcrawler and Havok struggle to do so, occupying social positions of alternate or even diminished masculinity in the eyes of the discourse of hegemonic masculinity.

Starting simply, then, Kurt Wagner/Nightcrawler is a character who finds his innate nature frequently at odds with the traditional masculine gender role. Born with blue fur and a tail, Kurt was abandoned by his mother in infancy and raised in a circus before being rescued, and recruited, by Charles Xavier/Professor X. In Kurt, Claremont offers us a character who is actively pressured by gender expectations for a superhero (both by others and himself). He is struggling to find a balance between who he is expected to be as a superhero, and who he is innately as a person. Unlike Cyclops or Wolverine, however, Kurt does not really struggle with self-acceptance, thus offering an evocative contrast to the ways in which self-acceptance factors into the complex identity negotiations that we see in both Cyclops and Wolverine.

Claremont's account for the origins of Nightcrawler (quoted in the chapter epigraph above) speaks to this impulse to depict a mutant for whom self-acceptance is a given. Nightcrawler's character arc throughout the Claremont run is thus more focused on his pursuit of social acceptance than it is on self-acceptance, which he seems to have already. In his first appearance in *Giant-Size X-Men* no. 1 (Wein and Cockrum), he asks Xavier, "Can you help me be normal?" Xavier later asks him if he still wants to be normal after being chased by a lynch mob, to which Kurt replies, "Perhaps not. I want only to be a whole Kurt Wagner! If you can make me that, teacher, I will go with you" (*Deadly Genesis!* 4).

Of course, self-acceptance is not the only form of acceptance. Throughout the run thereafter, Claremont has Kurt/Nightcrawler deal with the bigotry and prejudice that come with being a visible minority, an arduous and exhausting process that requires endless vigilance and constant learning. Kurt likes Kurt, but that is not the end of his problems. He must learn to adopt coping methods, strategies for reaching out, a supportive network of friends, and even the capacity to cut toxic people out of his life. This portrayal runs contrary to a cultural myth that suggests self-acceptance is the end of the journey for people in an oppressed minority, a myth that denies the complexity of social realities, and unfairly puts the burden on the oppressed to alter their perception.

Kurt's pursuit of social acceptance can also be read as analogous to conflicts with racial prejudice. Darowski observes, for example, that "Nightcrawler introduces a new dimension to the series. A mutant who is identified at sight allows the mutant metaphor to be more closely aligned with a racial metaphor" (*X-Men* 66). Like Storm, then, Nightcrawler opens up a stronger possibility to explore the portrayal of gender from an intersectional perspective, at least symbolically. And indeed, Kurt's relationship to his masculinity is greatly defined by his grotesque physical appearance in terms of empowering him to deviate further (as a result of already being othered in a manner that might be analogous, again, to Donna Harraway's concept of cyborg feminism). Throw in Ramzi Fawaz's concept of queer mutanity, and Kurt becomes a capable character vehicle for exploring identity from the perspective of race, sexuality, nationality, disability (at times he requires technological intervention to function within society), and class (he grew up a poor orphan and circus performer). All of these factors inform Kurt's capacity to challenge gender roles, but that foundation of self-acceptance merged with his desire for social acceptance is highly relevant as a starting point for discussing his effeminate characteristics.[1] It is also relevant when considering how the fluid symbology of *X-Men* comics starts to overlap gender deviancy with mutant minority status.

Kurt's gender deviancy can once again be examined within a historical context. R. W. Connell, for example, identified the emergence of a new masculine archetype in the 1970s and 1980s, "a group of men who have attempted to reform their masculinity, in part because of feminist criticism. They are exactly the kind of 'soft' men scorned by the mythopoetic men's movement and other masculine revivalists" (120). As I will demonstrate, Kurt's embrace of softness is a key element of his character.

Multiple aspects of Kurt/Nightcrawler's representation project a diminished masculine presence. His power set adds a great deal to his gender-deviant portrayal. Though frequently used offensively, his ability to hide in shadows (later retconned away) and to teleport put him symbolically in the category of those who choose flight over fight. He kills only two nonhumanoids in the entirety of his tenure, and no humans. In contrast, Storm kills eight nonhumans and one human, and Wolverine dispatches five nonhumans and four humans throughout the Claremont run. Furthermore, Kurt's superpower disappears or fails more than that of any other X-Man. If loss of power is read metaphorically as a symbolic emasculation (a possibility explored in my reading of the Cyclops/Jean love scene), then Kurt stands out, tied as he is for the highest number of instances of being depowered with Colossus, a character who appears in significantly more issues than he does. Kurt's powers of teleportation fail him on thirteen separate occasions throughout the Claremont run. Adding to this pattern of diminution, Kurt's smaller stature and hunched form stand in sharp contrast to the puffed-chest alpha male postures of the other X-Men (fig. 6.1).

Though all these aspects contribute to the appearance of Kurt/Nightcrawler as perhaps subordinate, the character maintained a position of prominence in the series during the early years. He was originally designed by Dave Cockrum for a different series at DC Comics that never came to fruition but remained deeply close to his heart. His love of the character pushed Nightcrawler toward a certain centrality in both of Cockrum's runs on *UXM*. "He represented me in the book and I focused

**Fig. 6.1.** *Nightcrawler's stance in contrast with the stances of his X-Men teammates from* Fate of the Phoenix! (UXM, *vol. 1, no. 137*). *John Byrne, penciler.*

a lot of action around him whenever I could. I would have to drop a brick wall on him or something to get him out of the action" (qtd. in DeFalco 92). Indeed, in the first twelve issues of the Claremont run, Nightcrawler has more panel appearances and speech bubbles than any X-Man other than Cyclops (who was still functioning as the main focal character at that point). Kurt was a highly prominent character from the start, outpacing even Wolverine, the character who is perhaps most synonymous with the X-Men.

If we consider Kurt/Nightcrawler and Logan/Wolverine to be contrasting archetypes of masculinity at the start of the Claremont run (the newer masculinity that Connell speaks to, and the more traditional masculinity described extensively in the previous chapter), then the relationship between the two of them becomes richly symbolic. Claremont chose to render this duality in a noncompetitive manner, with Nightcrawler embracing a flirtatious, effeminate, "soft" masculinity, and Wolverine projecting a rugged, violent, primal masculinity. And instead of symbolic normalization through competition, Kurt and Logan admire, support, and reinforce each other's chosen gender roles.

This relationship between Kurt and Logan is clear even in their first appearances in *X-Men* comics. Unlike all of his other masculine counterparts, Kurt's first introduction (in Wein and Cockrum's *Giant-Size X-Men* no. 1) shows him being victimized—hounded by a mob of torch-carrying and pitchfork-wielding villagers. From the outset, he's characterized as prey, in sharp contrast to the more dominating male presences that we see in the introductions to Wolverine, who is introduced telling off and threatening a military bureaucrat; Thunderbird, who is introduced chasing down a wild bison; and Colossus, who is introduced rescuing his sister by destroying a runaway tractor. Sunfire and Banshee are briefly introduced through simple conversations, but Storm is first shown being worshipped as a goddess in Kenya. Of all the X-Men, Kurt/Nightcrawler is the only one who has to be rescued by Professor X. Still speaking to that position of prominence, however, we should note that Kurt is the first new X-Man to be introduced in the story.

When Claremont began writing *UXM* with issue no. 94, he frequently placed Kurt in the role of a nurturer to other members of the team. For example, in *UXM* no. 98 he is seen checking in on Cyclops, who has been overworking himself: "Cyclops . . . Scott. You've been working four days straight with no rest, precious little food . . . you're burning yourself out my friend" (*Merry Christmas, X-Men* 31). The next issue sees Kurt worrying about Colossus's anxiety about traveling to outer space. The depth of his empathy in this issue is considerable. First, Kurt is seen checking in on Colossus, then we see him contemplating Colossus's anxiety, and then finally we see him checking back with Colossus to make sure he is recuperating successfully (*Deathstar, Rising!* 7–10). In both scenes, Claremont establishes Kurt as sensitive and compassionate—which is a noble portrayal, but one that is at odds with traditional masculine gender roles. As Connell notes, men are constrained by a "taboo on free expression of emotions, especially vulnerability" (247).

In that same issue, Cyclops seems to impugn Nightcrawler's masculinity (at least metaphorically) during a battle with robots. "Thanks for the assist, Nightcrawler—I couldn't have held my breath much longer, but you're not in a circus anymore, mister. That kind of flamboyance can cost us if you're not careful." The association of the word *flamboyance* as a signifier of both femininity and homosexuality is perhaps significant here. Nightcrawler responds to Cyclops assertively, saying, "I have been a showman all my life, Cyclops . . . it is in my blood, and I'm not about to change for you or anyone!" (*Deathstar, Rising!* 22). As he does so, he defends Cyclops from yet another robot attack, a move that can perhaps be seen to symbolically emasculate Cyclops in reciprocity for his attempt to verbally emasculate Kurt.

Returning to the project data sets, certain patterns of the Claremont run support the interpretation of Kurt/Nightcrawler as anomalous in his conformity to certain masculine roles. In the first twelve issues of the Claremont run, Nightcrawler has 171 speech bubbles (the most of any of the new *X-Men* characters) and 45 thought bubbles (behind only Storm, who beats him by one). This is in sharp contrast to more traditionally masculine teammates such as Colossus (117 speech bubbles, 14 thought bubbles) and Wolverine (143 speech bubbles, 15 thought bubbles). Thus, in contrast to the stoic "I speak with my hands" ideal of comics masculinity, Kurt is presented as contemplative and deliberate.

As mentioned earlier, this portrayal of Kurt/Nightcrawler becomes even more poignant when juxtaposed with that of Logan/Wolverine. Their relationship is considered an iconic example of brotherly friendship, but also a subversively queer one. In fact, as of February 12, 2020, the popular fan-fic site Archive of Our Own had 326 stories listed under the "Wolverine/Nightcrawler relationship" tag. In contrast, only 248 stories are listed for the Wolverine/Jean Grey romance. If nothing else, this establishes a cultural reception of their relationship that invites romantic speculation from readers; they are "shippable."

We first see the Wolverine/Nightcrawler relationship really develop in *Something Wicked This Way Comes!* (*UXM* no. 139) in the immediate aftermath of the *Dark Phoenix Saga*. When Logan decides to return to Canada to make peace with Department H, his former employer, Professor X suggests that he not go alone. Logan chooses Kurt as chaperone. When next we see the duo, they are squatting in the house of Logan's old friend Heather Hudson, waiting for her. As she throws open the door, we see Logan stretched out with his legs on the table in full repose, sipping a can of beer. Kurt, in contrast, panics at the sight of Heather and drops his own beverage, a bottle of soda. The contrast in the characters' demeanors and drink choices reflects a pluralistic portrayal of masculinity, building a foil relationship between the two characters in which Wolverine is the confident, hypermasculine rugged man, and Nightcrawler is his soft foil.

This contrast is often emphasized to comedic extent, such as later in the story, when the shape-shifter Snow Bird suddenly appears behind Nightcrawler as a polar bear. Nightcrawler comically exclaims, "Yikes!" before jumping onto Wolverine's back for protection. Wolverine chastises him, saying, "Get offfa me willya? Before these bozos laugh themselves to death," to which Kurt replies, "only if it's safe" (*Something Wicked This Way Comes!* n.p.). The issue ends with Nightcrawler being ambushed by Wendigo (a Hulk-like monster in the context of this story). As it approaches, Kurt meekly calls out, "Help!" set in a diminutive font size to emphasize his helplessness (n.p.).

Adding to the developing foil effect in this issue is the rugged nature of the story and setting itself. Wolverine is tracking a monster in the northern

wilderness along the shores of Hudson Bay. It is the kind of hypermasculine setting that we see in Fletcher Hanks's *Big Red McLane*, and Wolverine
is completely in his element. Nightcrawler, in sharp contrast once again, is
a fish out of water throughout the entire story.

Returning to the concept of victory in violent combat as a masculinized trope, the Kurt/Logan relationship also features a tradition of
one-sided sparring. *UXM* no. 148 (*Cry, Mutant!*) establishes that one of
the rituals of their friendship involves training in the forest behind the
mansion, where the two take turns hunting each other, with the loser buy-
ing the beer. In this first depiction of the ritual, we see Wolverine dominate, frighten, and then, as Logan, chastise Kurt after he finds and nearly
claws Nightcrawler in an animalistic display of dominance: "Scared you,
didn't I? Serves you right, Kurt, after making a dumb-butt move like that."
As they walk back to the mansion, Logan remarks, "I really enjoy these
improvised training sessions a heckuva lot more than our workouts in the
Danger Room. Especially since the loser buys the beer. How many cases
do you owe me now, anyway?" (n.p.).

Their relationship dynamic is further reflected in Wolverine's perspective on Kurt's visual duality. Nightcrawler's appearance is somewhat variable in the hands of specific artists, but he tends to run the gamut between
looking like a demon and looking like an elf, and he is referred to as both
in various stories, with "fuzzy elf" a term of affection that Wolverine himself adopts during their Wendigo adventure, in which Logan refers to Kurt
simply as "Fuzzy" (n.p.). He also refers to Kurt extensively as "misfit" or
"elf." This further characterizes their relationship as affectionate, but also
as condescending and/or patronizing.

On the opposite side is Kitty Pryde, a character who initially struggles
to feel comfortable around Kurt because of his demonic appearance. In
*UXM* no. 139, she thinks to herself, "This is crazy! Each time I see Nightcrawler, I flinch. I can't seem to help myself. I want to like him, but he
looks so ... different. He gives me the creeps" (*Something Wicked This Way
Comes!* n.p.). In the next panel Kurt again demonstrates his emotional intelligence by actually picking up on Kitty's unspoken discomfort. "Kitty's
hiding her feelings well, but I know I still make her nervous. I've tried to
break the ice between us, but so far nothing's worked." Undaunted, he tells
himself, "I'll simply have to keep trying. I like her too much to give up"
(n.p.). In this instance, Nightcrawler is again showcasing an interest in relationships, something that comics scholar Roger Sabin specifically identifies as a defining attribute of the highly gendered pre-1980s approach to
writing female comic book characters (86–91).

Furthermore, Nightcrawler's relationship with Kitty is platonic, whereas strong male-female relationships in comics at that time were almost exclusively romantic in nature. The result is an important cross-gender friendship, as articulated by comics scholar Anna Peppard.

> Chris Claremont laid the groundwork for Kitty Pryde and Kurt Wagner/Nightcrawler to develop one of the *X-Men* franchise's most complex and sustained cross-gender friendships. Kitty's initial fear of Kurt compels intersectional explorations of how different mutations are perceived differently, even by other mutants, and inspires Kurt to reflect on his ingratiating approach to acceptance. Their relationship has several important turning points, including a buddy adventure in space (Uncanny X-Men no. 155–157), and a second space adventure in which Kitty (inadvertently) takes her first sentient life, to save Kurt (Uncanny no. 163). Kitty befriending Kurt becomes symbolic of her developing maturity and social consciousness; her iconic defenses of the mutant cause in Uncanny no. 210 and God Loves, Man Kills extend from her devotion to Kurt. Relevant to the former: Kitty is Jewish; Kurt is German. In the Claremont-penned tie-in Excalibur, Kitty propels Kurt's own maturation. The series opens with Kitty admonishing Kurt's senseless bravado after he is nearly impaled fighting robotic pirates. With the other X-Men seemingly dead, Kurt must grow up; for Kitty, he does. Their relationship is largely devoid of sexual tension. Kitty is one of the few X-women Kurt (a notorious flirt) never tries to romance, except, interestingly, in a comedic guise within a bedtime story Kitty tells to Illyana ("Kitty's Fairy Tale," Uncanny no. 153). In post-Claremont stories, Kitty and Kurt continue to function as emotional outlets for each other. On numerous occasions, their interactions inspire important confessions of vulnerability, often leading to character growth (and tearful hugs). Individually, each character has often been framed as a "soul" of the X-Men. But they arguably communicate the franchise theme even better through their friendship, their heroism emerging through a model of found family grounded in intersectional empathy. ("Chris Claremont laid the groundwork" n.p.)

Arguably, the ability to have intimate platonic relationships with women is, in itself, a deviation from the traditional masculine gender roles in 1970s comics, although the manner in which Kurt interacts with Kitty through shared interests in fashion, stories, and nonsexual hugging also speaks to Kurt's portrayal as gender deviant by the standards of his time, medium, and genre.

Kurt is not, however, platonic in all of his relationships with women, and seeing how the portrayal of his sexuality deviates from traditional gender roles contributes to the character's broader gender deviancy. Comics are famous for creating what Bukatman refers to as "simple adolescent masturbatory fantasies" (65). He is here referring to the male gaze and the representation of women in comics, a topic that is well covered by both Carolyn Cocca and Lillian S. Robinson in their respective texts. In these works, the conclusion is that rendering characters as a sexual spectacle for the audience is a process that is disproportionately gendered. And yet Nightcrawler moves against this grain in a notable instance by being subjected to (at an extradiegetic level) and by subjecting himself to (at the diegetic level) being consumed as a sexual spectacle.

As noted by Luce Irigaray, "there is a price to pay for being the agents of exchange: male subjects have to give up the possibility of serving as commodities themselves" (575). Exceptions to this gender rule are rare, particularly in North American comics of the time. Yet, in *UXM* no. 168 (*Professor Xavier Is a Jerk!*), Paul Smith created a drawing of Nightcrawler (fig. 6.2) in homage to Burt Reynolds's 1972 *Cosmopolitan* nude centerfold, a famous image of masculine commodification that has been credited with inspiring Doug Lambert to create *Playgirl* magazine the following year. According to Reynolds,

> Although no one had ever shown a naked man in a magazine before, Helen [Gurley Brown, editor of *Cosmopolitan*] believed women have the same "visual appetites" as men, who'd been looking at naked women in *Playboy* since 1953. She wanted the same prerogative for women. It would be a milestone in the sexual revolution, and she said I was the one man who could pull it off. (*Cosmopolitan* n.p.)

In this sense, the image that Smith is paying homage to had a clear purpose: equalizing the male gaze and female gaze in magazine periodical spreads. Drawing on that image could thus be seen to potentially do the same thing for comics, where the sexual commodification of men has been more rare. In this scene, however, Nightcrawler is offered up in a visual-sexual context for erotic consumption.

Supporting this interpretation is the narration by Kurt/Nightcrawler's girlfriend, Amanda, thus presenting Kurt as an offering to the sexualizing gaze of a depicted character and the reader at the same time. Kurt's

**Fig. 6.2.** *Nightcrawler presents his body as a gift to Amanda Sefton in* Professor Xavier Is a Jerk! *(UXM, vol. 1, no. 168). Paul Smith, penciler.*

dialogue further endorses the proposition he is making: "I know you have my 'bamf' doll to keep you company and protect you, but I thought—this being Christmas and all—you might, for a change, prefer the real thing." The sexual association with the "bamf" doll is potent given its positioning in the scene: in front of Kurt's genitalia. Similarly, the foregrounded image of a gift-wrapped box (thus recapitulating the presentation of Kurt's body as a gift) as well as an erect bottle of champagne chilling in an ice bucket just above Kurt's abdomen contribute to his sexualization in this image. Off-panel, Amanda replies, "Yum!"—a potentially apt response for a metaphor of consumption (*Professor Xavier Is a Jerk!* n.p.).

The next issue of *UXM* features a tightly muscled Nightcrawler teleporting around the city naked in order to rescue his former teammate Angel. Thus, again we see Kurt functioning as a sex symbol, both in the unified display of flesh and super heroics, and in the narrative trope of "oops, I lost my clothes," one long-entrenched in comics history with regard to female characters (such as Wally Wood's *Sally Forth*) and a tradition that makes it quite frequently into Marvel comics of the time with regard to superheroines.

In a piece for The Middle Spaces website, Anna Peppard reads a different Nightcrawler scene composed by Claremont (from *Excalibur* no. 4) in an erotic light, specifically noting the complex relationship between Kurt's gender and his appeal to an erotic gaze.

Nightcrawler's especially visible, especially fantastical difference makes him an especially appealing site of erotic affiliation. Even though Nightcrawler, like other male superheroes, is rarely presented as an erotic spectacle the same way a female character like Meggan is, his body is inherently gender fluid, every masculine characteristic paired with a connotatively feminine counterpoint. His power is conveyed through acrobatic flexibility, his vampire fangs are domesticated by his iconic smile, and his tail both thrusts and squeezes, coiling around his own body or the hilts of swords, but also, sometimes, around the waist or thigh of a friend or lover. I've also thought entirely too much about the fact that Kurt's hardbody is literally soft, all those taut muscles coated by a thin layer of fur that, canonically, approximates the texture of velvet. (I bet that feels better than good.) ("Blue Becomings" n.p.)

In Peppard's reading, Kurt's gender fluidity, and, indeed, monstrosity actually enhance his erotic appeal.

Finally, on the subject of Kurt, we can integrate him into the discussion on the connection between leadership and the male gender role because he was briefly made leader of the field team midway through Claremont's run. This topic was explored in previous chapters with the characters of Cyclops, Storm, and Psylocke, and Kurt/Nightcrawler provides a particularly poignant contrast to Ororo/Storm. Whereas Storm succeeded in the role, despite being a woman, Nightcrawler fails, despite being a man, thus offering an intriguing contrast.

In Nightcrawler's first go as team captain (*UXM* no. 193), Claremont portrays him as woefully and tragically incapable. In a short span of time, the X-Men suffer multiple injuries and setbacks, despite the fact that their foes are four minors. This leads Kurt to question his capacity extensively. Twice in the span of three pages he wonders out loud if the bad results would have happened to previous leaders: "Would this have happened if Storm or Cyclops were in charge?!" (*Warhunt 2* n.p.). Then, in the next issue (*UXM* no. 194) Logan contemplates Kurt's struggles, thinking, "Nightcrawler's havin' a hard time cuttin' it as boss—he ain't a natural like Cyclops an' Storm. He's tryin' his best but he's pushing himself too hard, scared stiff of the cost of failure" (*Juggernaut's Back in Town!* n.p.). He even contemplates replacing Kurt with Kitty, a fifteen-year-old, as official leader. It never comes to this though because Cyclops comes out of retirement to lead the team until Storm returns to challenge him for the leadership role in *Duel* (*UXM* no. 201), published in 1985.

Kurt would leave the team in the wake of the *Mutant Massacre* cross-over event, but Claremont then made him a major character in *Excalibur*, a British-based *X-Men* spinoff. In his time with *Excalibur*, Kurt would become a competent leader, as well as a romantic rival for the hypermasculine Captain Britain. In Alan Davis's illustrations, Kurt stands fully upright and adopts a highly masculine fashion style including cable-knit sweaters and turtlenecks. Although this can be seen as a natural development for the character, in keeping with the aims and ambitions of the *UXM* version, it appears that Kurt's gender fluidity may have been significantly reduced in the *Excalibur* years, but that is a much larger subject of study than I can address here.

More immediately, Kurt's departure from *UXM* leaves Logan without a soft foil, but that role is quickly filled when Claremont has former X-Man Alex Summers/Havok join the team just as Kurt departs. Havok was originally introduced as an *X-Men* character in the 1960s, and he joined the team shortly thereafter, before leaving with the arrival of the *New X-Men* in the aftermath of *Giant-Size X-Men* no. 1. From there, he was effectively retired, though he popped up in the series as an occasional guest star before returning to active duty in the wake of the *Mutant Massacre* event.

Through Havok, Claremont would continue to build on many of the ways that Nightcrawler spoke to masculinity as a concept, though with greater emphasis on the harrowing impact that it can have on nonconforming individuals. Claremont's Havok stands out for his innate pacifism (despite his extraordinary power), his emotional vulnerability, and his tragic inability to live up to the superhero ideal (as well as the various entanglements of that ideal, such as masculinity).

Havok is reintroduced in a prologue story in *UXM* no. 218, in which the Jeep he is in is run off a road in New Mexico, thus interrupting his otherwise idyllic life with his love, Lorna Dane (also a former X-Man, Polaris). Claremont immediately adds a grim portent to his pastoral portrayal through the narration:

> A special breed calls this desert home. Even rarer are those who are happy here. Two such are Alex Summers and Lorna Dane. He's a geologist, her field's archeology. He studies the land, while she explores the history of those who walked upon it. It's a good life that's about to end. (*Charge of the Light Brigade* n.p.)

Of minor note here, as we might argue that driving an open-topped Jeep through the desert has a certain masculine association, is the fact that Lorna is the driver.

Claremont then establishes Havok's reluctant use of power (in this case, superpower). As he uses his plasma beams to stop a boulder from striking the wrecked Jeep, the narrator informs us, "He's a mutant, born different from most other people—possessing the power to metabolize cosmic radiation and unleash it as beams of focused plasma. It's a gift he'd usually prefer to do without" (n.p.). Indeed, Havok's extreme reluctance toward the superhero mission is a defining attribute of his character, and one that can be seen to intersect with his performance of masculinity in compelling ways. As Lorna/Polaris uses her powers to right the Jeep, Havok tells her to take it easy, to which she replies, "I'm not a porcelain doll, you chauvinist worm." His response is to correct her: "Pig. Chauvinist pig." Polaris, however, corrects his correction: "Worm, buster. I like pigs" (n.p.).

This playful exchange establishes their dynamic, but also invests in that dynamic a self-awareness of gender roles and expectations, priming the reader, potentially, to interpret Havok within the context of the same self-aware 1980s "soft man" politics that define Nightcrawler. The idyllic nature of his relationship with Polaris also adds an element of endorsement to these politics. The result, in this case, is a healthy relationship in which gender roles are both fluid and open to interrogation.

Unfortunately, just as the narration foreshadowed, that healthy relationship is over. In the next issue (*UXM* no. 219), Havok awakes from a nightmare in their New Mexico home with his power raging out of control. He streams out of bed and out the front door, praying that the airspace above him is free of planes before blasting his pent-up energy into the sky at such force that he thinks, "They'll see my glow in Taos and Santa Fe—and probably, in time, all across the Milky Way. A man, flashing bright as any star." The outburst is powerful enough to fuse the desert sand beneath his feet into glass. As Lorna runs to comfort him with a blanket, Alex falls into shock and starts crying, then tries to apologize. "I'm sorry. I didn't mean I try to keep under control it's so hard I'm so scared it isn't fair why me why me?!" (*Where Duty Lies* 5–6). In this scene, Alex's relationship to power (and thus to masculinity) is dramatically rendered: he is unable to harness (or even control) his superpower and is instead victimized by it.

In the aftermath, Alex decides that he must journey to visit the X-Men. Lorna presumes to come with him, but Alex, acting somewhat chauvinistically, refuses. This is the other aspect of his character that Claremont frequently brings to light: though often portrayed as more effeminate than his masculine counterparts, Alex frequently falls into aspirations of archetypal masculinity, aspirations that almost always blow up in his face, so to speak. He wants to be the macho man's man, but he is not capable of performing it.

As Alex/Havok runs off solo on a mission to find the X-Men, Claremont portrays how far in over his head he is. As he searches for the X-Men, Havok decides to stealthily trail Magneto through the sewer tunnels in order to find them. (At this point, Magneto is operating as an ally of the X-Men.) Havok's internal monologue, delivered as he makes several mistakes, highlights his unheroic nature:

> I don't want to die or even get hurt, so why do I continually put my life on the line? Masked by the chattering lightshow of the subway's passing, I blast the alcove and give the wall a hearty shove. [He then plunges into an abyss.] Smart move, Sherlock. I grab for anything. I get lucky. Sort of. A thousand years later—when breath and heart are back to normal and I don't hurt quite so much I start down. (*Where Duty Lies* 15–16)

He then finds his way to a secret meeting of the X-Men, but accidentally blasts the X-Woman Rogue (nearly killing her) before sprinting away, thinking, "I run for my life" (18).

Transitioning from one failure to another, Claremont shifts the action back to Lorna in New Mexico, where she is now under assault by a mutant terrorist group, the Marauders, who are, of course, taking advantage of the fact that she is alone. With a sense of Havok's further failure in play, the scene switches back to Manhattan, where we next see Havok nearly kill another X-Woman, Dazzler this time, due again to a lack of control, narrating his failure: "I react without thinking, from an instinct that terrifies me. The plasma bolt leaps from my fingers before I've even realized I've fired. I'd give anything to call it back. But I can't" (*Where Duty Lies* 20).

Throughout the issue, penciler Bret Blevins renders Havok in prone postures (fig. 6.3) to help symbolize his timidity and incompetence in a manner that reflects some of Dave Cockrum's portrayals of Nightcrawler discussed earlier. As an additional point of contrast, whereas Nightcrawler is rescued from a murderous mob by an offer of admission to the X-Men, Havok's murderous mob is the X-Men themselves, who actively contemplate murdering him after he overhears the X-Men's plan to fake their deaths. Havok laments his fear, saying, "I don't know what scares me more, Psylocke's suggestion or the fact that Storm takes it seriously. I think of Lorna, wonder if I'll ever see her again" (*Where Duty Lies* 22). In this,

**Fig. 6.3.** *Havok cowers in front of the other X-Men in* Where Duty Lies (UXM, *vol. 1, no. 219*). *Bret Blevins, penciler.*

he is again placed in the position of harmless prey, the notion being that if they want to kill him, he lacks the power to stop them. He is at the mercy of their whims, so he offers to join them instead. After consultation with Magneto, they accept.

Havok's struggles continue in the next issues. During his first mission with the team in *UXM* no. 221, he is chastised by Wolverine for reacting to a mental attack. He falls to his knees, screaming, "Wolverine—my lord—I'm burning! It's more than I can stand!" Wolverine (still standing) thinks, "Figured Havok to be cast from the same mold as his big brother, Cyclops. What if I'm wrong, suppose he can't hack it as an X-Man?!" (*Death by Drowning!* 14). In this scene, we actually have the two key contrasts in play that define Havok: his inability to be like his brother (or perhaps his brother's shadow) and his inability to be like his contemporary teammate Wolverine. The next issue (*UXM* no. 222) (continuing the same conflict) ends with Alex weeping alone on a rooftop (*Heartbreak!* 22).

These early portrayals establish Claremont's use of Havok to undermine the traditional superhero bravado, an aspect with clear connections to hegemonic masculinity. Havok would eventually become marginally effective as an X-Man, but he always remains aloof and introspective—someone who does not really fit into the found family of the team, but exists peacefully enough on the periphery. This was somewhat true metatextually as well, with Havok rarely taking an important role in individual storylines. This would change, however, with the *Inferno* crossover event in *UXM* nos. 239–243.

In the build-up to the *Inferno* storyline, Havok kindles an affair with Madelyne Pryor, his brother's estranged wife, thus bringing to the surface the extent to which he feels that he is living in his brother's shadow. His affair with Madelyne is arguably a way to transgress that, but when that relationship proves to be exploitative of Havok, he is once again left defeated, having chosen sides (under the influence of sorcery) with the enemy.

Shortly thereafter, Havok (in a daze) uses his powers to assist Storm in a battle with the airship of the villain Nanny. Havok is recovering from a fight at this point and fires his plasma beam in confused desperation. The result is the downing of the airship, but also the death of Storm, who appears to have been killed by Havok in a friendly fire incident.[2] In the aftermath of that terrible mistake, Havok is seen drinking and sulking in the basement of the X-Men's Australia base. He directly compares himself to Wolverine, asking aloud, "[W]ould things have ended any differently if Wolverine had been here? All this time, I was so sure that in a crunch I could handle myself as good as him. Maybe even better" (*The Dane Curse* 4). He ends up taking out his anger and frustration on a TV monitor he's watching but can't even succeed in that petulant act, and his blast ricochets, knocking him to the floor, unconscious, preventing him from receiving the call for help from his former lover Lorna/Polaris, which arrives seconds later.

In his following pursuit of Polaris, it is clear that Havok has lost his delusions of heroism. He threatens to torture a member of the villainous Zaladane's forces for information while espousing hypermasculine ideals. "Psylocke's a lady, she has scruples," he says. "I'm not so forgiving. How 'bout I sizzle you, say a limb at a time, till you decide to cooperate? Heat's so intense, the stumps'll instantly cauterize, so you won't bleed to death. Tough guy like you, bet you last a long time" (*The Dane Curse* 20). Psylocke (a telepath) reacts in horror: "my lord—Havok—you're serious!?!" Already emulating Wolverine's previous behavior, Havok then uses a Wolverine line on the victim of his interrogation: "your choice, your funeral" (20). This mimicry of Wolverine's voice further solidifies Havok's place within the X-Men masculinity hierarchy as articulated in this and other chapters. As Kurt/Nightcrawler does, Alex/Havok aspires to be like

Wolverine. He's just not very good at it. The fact that Wolverine himself does not want to be Wolverine, in large part due to the collateral damage he suffers in maintaining a hypermasculine ideal, adds some potential dramatic irony to Havok's emulation of him.

After Havok's attempted infiltration of Zaladane's fortress fails, a strong female villain mocks him openly as her goons easily defeat him. His attackers refer to him with the pejorative term "boy," then hold him back as Zaladane turns her attention toward the captive Polaris: "Provide him a ringside seat. I don't want him to miss a moment" (*The Shattered Star* 6–7). Havok is next seen weeping openly and screaming "Lorna!" as Zaladane siphons Lorna's power in a painful spectacle. Claremont's narration describes Havok's cries as "anguished, heartsick sobs" (8), again dramatizing his symbolic emasculation. In response to a trauma, he attempts to emulate Wolverine's masculine ideals, but he fails spectacularly.

Claremont juxtaposes all of this with another superpower gender reversal. Polaris's superpowers are altered in the exchange with Zaladane, replacing her feminine point-and-pose powers (she controls magnetism) with increased size and super strength, powers that are traditionally masculine. She puts these to use in freeing herself and Havok from Zaladane's prison before aggressively planting a kiss on the helplessly dangling Havok, a kiss that plays, visually, on gender-swapped roles as she thinks to herself, "Gracious—I'm taller than he is!" (*The Shattered Star* 19).

By the next issue (*UXM* no. 251), it is Havok who suggests the X-Men should disband. "Well, I've had it, folks. I've paid my dues—we all have, with the scars to prove it. I say, the time's come to call it quits" (*Fever Dream* 17). Havok has had enough, and with that, and a little psychic push from Psylocke, the X-Men all disappear through the Siege Perilous, as described in chapter 3.

All told, Havok is portrayed as an individual who aspires to a superheroic paradigm of masculinity—the same paradigm that his brother Cyclops learned to distrust for the sake of his well-being, and the same paradigm that Wolverine, whom Havok idolizes, has to consciously avoid embodying for fear of losing all of his humanity. Whereas Cyclops and Wolverine represent the undesirability of conformity to a traditional masculine gender role, Havok portrays the fundamental impossibility of that same conformity, thus establishing the artifice behind the concept of hegemonic masculinity: the ideals are not just undesirable, they are also unattainable. Alex's failure is not just tragic, it is revelatory, and in contrast to Nightcrawler, whose life and character arc are defined by an empowering gender nonconformity, Havok can only ever be disappointed in himself.

**Fig. 6.4.** *Havok is rescued by Polaris in* The Shattered Star *(UXM, vol. 1, no. 250). Marc Silvestri, penciler.*

We can see this sense of perpetual failure come to a head, somewhat, in an issue that showcases Havok's relationship within the broader cosmology of the X-Men. Bringing this discussion of masculine gender roles to a close then, the issue that follows *Ladies Night* (discussed in chapter 3) is simply and similarly titled *Men!* Like *Ladies Night*, this issue features a direct send-up of gender-based rituals, with the male X-Men spending a night at a roadhouse playing poker, holding drinking competitions, and brawling. The issue is completely farcical, even featuring some insightful autocriticism,[3] and it specifically showcases the spectrum of gender nonconformity displayed by the team members.

Interestingly, the issue was guest-penciled by a young Rob Liefeld, an artist whose emphasis on excess and highly gendered bodies would become the focus of important works of comics scholarship, such as Bart Beaty and Benjamin Woo's *The Greatest Comic Book of All Time* and Anna Peppard's "The Power of the Marvel(ous) Image." Beaty and Woo, in particular, note that "Liefeld's aesthetic, like that of Jack Kirby before him, is one of excess" (79), where gender is overdetermined to a degree that "the men are conventionalized signs of strength and power, the women arbitrary signifiers of an abstract non-functional sexiness" (80). We might thus infer a bit of irony to Liefeld showing up as a guest penciler on this of all issues.

Liefeld's cover for *Men!* shows the current male members of the X-Men (Colossus, Longshot, Havok, and Wolverine) surrounded by guns pointing at them. Instead of showing fear, Wolverine says, "Be a shame if something bad happens to my nice new jacket!" Although the use of this specific implicature can be traced back to gangster films of the 1920s (thus aligning Logan/Wolverine with yet another masculine archetype), the circumstances surrounding this image create the broader implication that Wolverine has no concern for the guns pointed at him, only for his jacket. He does not even see the attackers as a threat to his well-being. His hypermasculinity here is ironic, of course, given the humorous nature of the story that follows, and the text bubble on the cover that precedes it, which has Colossus, the armored giant of the team, exclaim, "Ulp! We're surrounded by hostile aliens!" By the 1960s, "ulp" was already an outdated comics expression, one that, ironically, harkens back to Silver Age comics tropes. Thus, the tongue-in-cheek aspect of the issue is readily manifest on the cover page.

The story that unfolds in *Men!* is a satire of the 1988 DC Comics' *Invasion* crossover event that established DC's version of superhero mutation through the detonation of the "gene bomb," paving the way for DC to directly imitate the *X-Men* franchise. This turf war with a rival publisher helps set the tone for the sendup that unfolds in the issue.

The first page opens with an alien invader shouting, "MEN! For those who complained of having no more new worlds to conquer, I give you the planet earth!" The exclamation immediately associates masculinity with the imperialist drive to conquer. The alien also tells them to "go forth" (1–2), which may be an allusion to Tennyson's phrase "Arise, go forth, and conquer as of old" from "The Passing of Arthur," in his epic poem *Idylls of the King*. It is also telling that the audience being addressed (revealed on the next page) features a wide variety of characters exhibiting feminine physical traits, most notably breasts; addressing that audience as "MEN!" reflects ignorance at best, and patriarchal arrogance at worst.

We might also note that the crowd is filled with pop culture characters such as the Xenomorph (from *Alien*); Jabba the Hutt (from *Return of the Jedi*); Hawkman (from *Justice League*); and Yoda, Bobba Fett, and Darth Vader (all from *Empire Strikes Back*), among others. Although this might simply be reference comedy, the idea that the masculinist imperial invaders are populated with a number of geek cultural icons does open up the possibility of reading the discourse of hegemonic masculinity in geek culture as becoming integrated in the critique of masculinity that the issue performs. This would align with the arguments of scholars Lori Kendall and Ron Eglash, who both perceive geek culture to be deeply integrated with gender roles.

As the story transitions from aliens to the X-Men, we get a full-page splash of Havok staring at the X-Men's surveillance system, watching all of his teammates, including Storm, who is showering naked. The only X-Man not visible is Wolverine. Havok notes, "Shoot. Little runt's disabled his scanners again. This is getting to be a royal pain" (*Men!* 4). On the next page we see Wolverine sneak up behind Havok and grab him by the shoulder, exclaiming, "So are you, boy." Havok protests, asking how long Wolverine has been spying on him, to which he replies, "Nice choice o' words. I got the same question" (6). In light of the issue's themes and its exploration of a masculine mentoring relationship, having Wolverine call Havok out on his surveillance is telling. His voyeuristic behavior aligns with Susan Sontag's reading of photographic observation and possession as both phallic and imperial (a key thesis from her landmark work *On Photography*), and it may also hold the potential to be read as metatextual in the form of Havok's enactment of the gaze of the male comics reader; notably, the surveillance monitors are arranged in a grid to look like a comics layout.

This scene also establishes the leitmotif of Wolverine calling Havok "boy" and Havok's angry response: "And by the way, 'Bub,' you call me boy again—!" (*Men!* 6). This recurs throughout the issue, emphasizing the hierarchical nature of the two X-Men's relationship. When Storm intervenes as the voice of authority, Havok storms off in frustration (just before Wolverine refers to him as "boy" again, this time to Storm). Wolverine decides that the men of the team need a vacation of their own, following in the footsteps of the *Ladies Night* adventure from the previous issue. He smiles and tells Storm, "What's good for the goose, darlin' ..." (7). In partially invoking that phrase, Wolverine makes an argument for the exclusivity of gender (male-female/goose-gander), but also for a form of unity in that the statement fundamentally implies that the goose and the gander react to stimuli in identical ways and are therefore (more or less) the same.

The next scene features Piotr/Colossus in a barber's chair as Alison/Dazzler (the most femme-presenting member of the team) applies makeup to his face, even as he protests, "Alison, men do not wear such things" (*Men!* 8). She dismissively says, "Oh pooh—men also don't have bodies of organic chrome steel"—as Colossus does (9). In this assertion, Dazzler is fundamentally arguing that being a mutant places Colossus outside of the very concept of hegemonic masculinity. He is already different as a result of his superpower and is therefore empowered to deviate from established gender norms. In this simple statement, Dazzler is projecting Fawaz's concept of "queer mutanity" in the canon.[4] Colossus seems to accept this. When the other male X-Men show up to retrieve him, Wolverine says, "Petey Pureheart better be ready." Colossus stands up to greet him, in full facial makeup, smiling broadly and declaring, "As much so, Tovarish, as I shall ever be. And comrade, smile when you call me that." Dazzler, arms outstretched in celebration at Colossus's side, declares, "Better living through Revlon, guys. Am I a marvel or what?" (9).

From there the men depart on their manly adventure, ending up in a roadhouse in Sydney, Australia. Once inside the bar, their night unfolds—featuring barfights, seductions, poker, drinking contests, and ultimately the defeat of an absurd alien invasion as the climactic assertion of masculine identity. The connection between this last rite and masculinity is particularly signaled by a reference to a memorable scene from the 1986 film *Crocodile Dundee*. Famously, the scene features an American mugger accosting the title character with a small switchblade. Crocodile Dundee responds by drawing out a much larger knife and uttering his famous line "That's not a knife; *that's* a knife!" The mugger retreats, symbolically emasculated by Dundee's much larger phallic symbol. In *Men!*, as the aliens open fire on their traitorous commander's attack ship, Havok says, "You fellas call those blasters? Those aren't blasters. This is a blaster" (23), before firing his superpower beams into the sky. As Havok casually walks away from the exploding wreckage, still holding his beer, he utters, "Now—what's all this about a 'conquest'?" having simply not noticed that earth was being invaded at all, thus symbolically emasculating the alien invasion force further.

On the final page of the issue, the male X-Men return home to find the women waiting for them, led by Storm, who remarks, "Ah-hem! It would appear you 'gentlemen' had yourselves a grand old time" (*Men!* 30). This characterization of Storm as a sort of den mother is very out of character, perhaps reflecting the satiric tone of the story. As Wolverine approaches her, he says, "Darlin' it was the best," before kissing his captain. The last two panels feature Storm sitting on a bench by herself contemplating what just happened: "That man! Those Men!" (30). This ending is difficult to interpret given the issue's satiric tone, but it does seem to reaffirm hegemonic masculinity if read straight. If read ironically, it can instead be seen to represent a form of camp, like Wolverine's over-the-top performance of the masculine gender role that his character has routinely rejected. This is likewise the case for Storm, who, based on prior portrayals (and particularly in interactions with Wolverine), would be highly unlikely to tolerate being forced into a subservient role.

All combined, Claremont's direct send-up of masculine bonding culture speaks most directly to the overarching gender interrogations of the series through the simple, lighthearted tone of the entire issue. Every aspect of male bonding in *Men!* is framed within a narrative of excess, farce, and persistent undermining. Indeed, it might be quite difficult to walk away from the issue and still see male gender roles as anything other than artifice within the *X-Men* franchise.

# A Legacy in Waiting

Claremont is one of the most important figures in comics history, a guy who basically bridges the gap between classic Marvel Silver Age stuff and the British invasion writers like Moore and Morrison. He's created more notable characters in comics than anyone other than Stan Lee/Kirby—and beyond that, has just written a lot of fantastic stories. Everyone points to the Dark Phoenix Saga, but he wrote an intensely personal, ever-changing fifteen-year epic story that still reads great to this day.

—PATRICK MEANEY, FROM AN INTERVIEW WITH JULIUS DARIUS

n their 2016 book *The Greatest Comic Book of All Time: Symbolic Capital and the Field of American Comic Books*, Bart Beaty and Benjamin Woo offer a revisionist perspective on the ways that our culture builds "the canon of American comic books" (5), with the stated aim of "trying to imagine the end of this comics world and the beginning of another" (16). In pursuing this interest, they use Pierre Bourdieu's work on "fields" to create a system of comics valuation (based on quadrants) that uses two variables: economic success and cultural success—commercial sales and "the esteem of influential cultural intermediaries" (13). Traditionally, of course, the entire field of comics scholarship and criticism focused on the latter. Indeed, being commercially successful might even be seen to diminish a work's claim to esteem; after all, if everyone likes it, it must not be that good, right?

This logic is both deeply flawed, and deeply familiar, to literary scholars. Even Shakespeare was considered populist in his time. Beaty and Woo's model is thus operating against the grain of centuries of economic and politically motivated snobbery. The Claremont run does not benefit from this kind of snobbery. *X-Men* was a sales juggernaut, producing more than a decade of best-selling comics. In Beaty and Woo's model, however, Chris Claremont's run achieves the rarest form of cultural capital: a financially lucrative story that is also deeply esteemed and already firmly entrenched in the North American comics canon. Thus, in concluding this book, I would like to speak to cultural capital in the form of influence and, through that, the potential power of Claremont's portrayals of gender to endure and to transmit, virally, throughout our culture.

Today, Marvel comics are populated by a rich world of female characters who are tough, charismatic, engaging, and relatable. In the right circles, we can also find male characters who are sensitive, sympathetic, nurturing, and open. In the decades that have passed since the Claremont run took the comics world by storm (and by Storm), the idea of binary gender has eroded somewhat. However, it was monolithic in the Marvel comics of the 1970s, when a twenty-five-year-old editorial assistant said, "Me, please," when the task of writing *UXM* suddenly became available. Progress has indeed been made through the contributions of countless authors, artists, and editors fighting against the grain of a particularly imbalanced medium within a patriarchal society. Claremont was, in a lot of ways, an important part of this progress—perhaps even taking an occasional leap along with a series of small, hard-fought steps.

Claremont's work has remained perpetually in print since his initial departure from Marvel comics. His impact has been much discussed, with various movements of the medium attributed (in some part) to his influence. Scholar Colin Smith describes how "Claremont first pioneered the ultra-soap content" of modern comics (n.p.). Roger Sabin notes how Claremont "established the 'fan comic' style" (159) that altered comics culture in the late 1970s. Esteemed French filmmaker Olivier Assayas credits Claremont with cultivating a "transgressive eroticism" in comics "which seemed to be much more daring than what Hollywood cinema wanted to explore back then" (qtd. in Franklin n.p.). We can also add in Claremont's cultivation of increased depth and complexity (pivotal elements of the comics-as-literature movement). Scholar Michael Campochiaro notes that, "Influenced by the success of Claremont's Uncanny X-Men, comics of the mid- to late-Bronze Age began weaving together intricate tapestries of both plot and character development that could sometimes take years to play out fully" ("Blue Beetle" n.p.).

Claremont's sphere of influence transcends this medium, though, often without due acknowledgment. As the inspiration for many of the stories told in the iconic *X-Men: The Animated Series*, Claremont received writing credit on sixteen episodes. He also received writing credits on the 2017–2019 FX TV series *Legion*, which focused on David Haller, another character Claremont created and cultivated during his run. Of course, he should have received writing credits on the films made of his iconic stories, such as Fox's billion-dollar *X-Men* franchise. He did not, but fans of the stories know whose imagination so many of these characters, plots, and details sprang from.

Long-form television (commonly associated with the modern binge-watching phenomenon) may owe Claremont a particular debt of gratitude. Joss Whedon's *Buffy the Vampire Slayer* cultivated a unique genre of continuous, comics-like, long-form storytelling, and the influence of *X-Men* on Whedon is well known. Whedon has acknowledged that Buffy was modeled on Claremont's Kitty Pryde character (qtd. in Armitage n.p.), and Whedon famously (and quite obviously) riffed on Claremont's *Dark Phoenix Saga* for an extended season 6 storyline in *Buffy*. Less discussed, however, are the many similarities between Claremont's character Illyana Rasputin and Whedon's character Connor, from the *Buffy* spinoff *Angel*. Connor appears as part of an extended storyline across multiple seasons of *Angel* with a backstory that is nearly identical to Illyana's—despite how far-fetched that backstory is. Similarly, the landmark Netflix series *Stranger Things* contains several winking references to the Claremont run, and it was described by media critic Alex Abad-Santos as "a love letter to Jean Grey" (n.p.). The presence of Claremont's influence on these iconic works of long-form television storytelling reflects the simple conclusion articulated by legendary cross-platform writer Neil Gaiman: "It is great to see Chris Claremont getting his dues. Modern tv owes so much to him" (@neilhimself).

Whatever the Claremont run accomplished, it accomplished while part of the epicenter of comics culture—not the margins. There is something very compelling, though perhaps difficult to express, in that orientation. The cultural capital of the Claremont run is difficult to quantify, but whatever Claremont had to say about our society's relationship to traditional gender roles, and whatever patterns or promises might emerge from this book, Claremont's ideas reached, and continue to reach (through a myriad of forms), a very large audience. Perhaps that is what this all boils down to: a constellation of gender roles, expectations, performances, and impacts, all elegantly articulated and widely disseminated in a simple story about superpowered beings sworn to protect a world that hates and fears them.

# Acknowledgments

This book could not have been possible without the great capability, compassion, and inspiration of Frederick Luis Aldama. His stewardship of the project was everything and I would never have completed this book without his efforts.

I am also deeply grateful to Becca, Sabrina, Lauryn, and Tristan for their hard work in building our dataset and infrastructure.

Thanks as well to Chris Gonzalez, Jim Burr, and the entire team at the University of Texas Press for their innumerable individual and collective efforts in bringing this project to fruition.

I would also like to thank St. Jerome's University for their steadfast support of my weird little comics projects and for the leadership, mentorship, and collegiality provided by so many of the people that I am honored to share a hallway with.

Thanks as well to the Social Sciences and Humanities Research Council of Canada for their generous financial support of my project and for their willingness to recognize and empower the cultivation of comics scholarship.

And thanks to my inner circle of comics nerds that I could always hit up to talk through ideas: to Anna, Laura, Matt, Mav, and Michael, I think these casual conversation pieces are forever undervalued in the way we assign authorship and accreditation, but it really does mean the world to have the sounding board you all provided me and the time and expertise that you freely gave.

# Notes

## Introduction. X-Women to Watch Out For

1. In order to isolate our sample, we decided not to include *UXM* issue nos. 94–96, which were plotted by Len Wein and Marv Wolfman. We also excluded *UXM* no. 279 because Claremont was unable to finish it, though he does receive credit.

2. Darowski notes that Jean's teammate Bobby Drake is younger than her, yet he still gets to be called Iceman rather than Iceboy (*X-Men* 45). Claremont would create a litany of female characters for Marvel comics, not once incorporating the words "girl" or "woman" in their code names.

3. Interestingly, Claremont named one of his most famous antiheroes Mystique in homage to Friedan's philosophy. Mystique is a capable and courageous shape-shifter terrorist who lives with her female partner, Destiny.

4. The repetitious pattern of superheroines losing their superpowers has been identified by Gail Simone as an aspect of "fridging," a practice in comics that subordinates female characters by sacrificing their characterization (or even existence) for the sake of establishing further motivation for a male counterpart character ("Women in Refrigerators" n.p.).

5. Consideration of ornamentality is the basis of "the sexy lamp test" (Helvie), a frequently cited alternative to the Bechdel test.

6. It must be noted here that Mulvey, in keeping with Freudian thought, sees visual pleasure as a defense mechanism in response to castration anxiety caused by the fundamental "lack" of the represented women. I do not, at this point, agree with the theory of castration anxiety as the root of all sexism in comics, but I recognize the potential merits of such an approach. It may be the case that a fear of castration is at play in comics texts, but that is not the subject of this project. As a literary scholar, I focus on the effect that Mulvey identifies, not the cause that she supposes creates it.

7. In film parlance, "the fourth wall" refers to the imaginary boundary between the audience and the fictional world being represented.

## Chapter 1. Jean, Moira, and the Archetypal "Claremont Woman"

1. Michael Campochiaro provides a more expansive definition of the Claremont Woman: "She's fiercely self-sufficient, extremely intelligent, highly skilled, and in a fight she only needs herself and her weapon or powers to mete out the appropriate level of justice" ("Word on a Wing" n.p.).

2. We should perhaps note as well that narratives of possession are identified by Hélène Cixous as innately femininized, for "being possessed is not desirable

for a masculine Imaginary, which would interpret it as passivity—a dangerous feminine position. It is true that a certain receptivity is 'feminine' " (43).

## Chapter 3. *Ladies Night* and the Second Generation of Claremont Women

1.  See Deman, "Busting Loose," for a full discussion of this character's redemption arc and its long-term impact on *UXM* comics of the era.

## Chapter 4. She Makes Him Nervous

1.  Neil Shyminsky notes that "Cyclops's whiteness does not register as a particular race so much as a lack of race. We are far more aware of what he is not—not black like Storm, not Jewish like Kitty Pryde—rather than what he *is*, and so he can be perceived as simply a human" ("Mutation" 161).
2.  For Lorde, the mythical norm is variable according to context, but "in America, this norm is usually defined as white, thin, male, young, heterosexual, Christian, and financially secure" (631).
3.  We also have to note that Cyclops's portrayal of masculinity is immediately altered with the new constitution of the team. Whereas the first team was composed of four white, male, American heroes, the new international team does not feature any characters who fit all of these categories save for Scott. Thus the various entanglements of masculinity with race and nationality are suddenly shifted.

## Chapter 5. Wolverine as Subversive Masculine Paradigm

1.  Though perhaps counterintuitive to an unfamiliar audience, the cowboy attire that Logan/Wolverine frequently sports is commonly worn in parts of Canada (notably in Saskatchewan and Alberta, where *X-Men* artist John Byrne was raised).
2.  A full account of this idea and the resistance it met can be found in Sean Howe's *Marvel Comics: The Untold Story*, p. 328.
3.  Ironically, the term *man* here is, of the two terms, more aligned with femininity in its detachment from violent and primitive impulses.
4.  Windsor-Smith would go on to define Wolverine's backstory in 1991 with the *Weapon X* stories from *Marvel Comics Presents* nos. 72–84.
5.  This story was published about two years after Donna Harraway's essay *Cyborg Manifesto*, and there are some intriguing intersections between Lady Deathstrike and Harraway's interpretation of the gender-neutralizing power of cyborg imagery.

6. Alternately, we could call this aristeia the fulfillment of what Bukatman describes as "the longing for orgasmic battle" (56), an idea that could perhaps be viable for all forms of aristeia.

## Chapter 6. A Spectrum of "Men"

1. Fawaz notes that when Kurt is shown his worst nightmare by the magic M'Kraan crystal, "the Crystal recognizes Nightcrawler's greatest fear as the disintegration of his bond with the X-Men into xenophobia and hatred" (161).
2. Only two years later would it be revealed to Havok that he had been fooled by Nanny, who deployed a Storm body decoy in order to trick the X-Men.
3. The best example of this is that the aliens have a weapon of mass destruction called "the Jean Bomb," which is just a clone of Jean Grey in a tube that will, we are told, "dissolve the most loving bonds, prompt brother to slay brother and boon companions to tear themselves apart" (*Men!* 8). This is Claremont referencing the extent to which Jean Grey has been used as an agent of conflict in *X-Men* stories over the years.
4. The association with chrome steel might also invite a comparison to Donna Harraway's seminal argument in *The Cyborg Manifesto*, which is that the cyborg body is empowered to deviate from gender norms. Colossus is not a cyborg, of course, but he certainly looks like one, and since his aesthetic and its effect on what society expects from him as a man are the subject of the exchange, there is a greater validity to the comparison.

# References

Abad-Santos, Alex. "*Stranger Things* Is a Love Letter to the X-Men's Jean Grey." Vox, 5 Aug. 2016, https://www.vox.com/2016/8/5/12375808/stranger-things -xmen-134-jean-grey.

Abbott, Megan. Introduction. *The Street Was Mine: White Masculinity in Hardboiled Fiction and Film Noir*, edited by M. Abbott, Palgrave, 2002, pp. 1–20.

Aeschylus. *The Oresteia*. Edited by Robert Fagles, Penguin Books, 1998.

*Alien*. Directed by Ridley Scott, performances by Sigourney Weaver, Ian Holm, and John Hurt, 20th Century Fox, 1980.

Alimahomed, Sabrina. "Thinking Outside the Rainbow: Women of Color Redefining Queer Politics and Identity." *Social Identities*, vol. 16, no. 2, 2010, pp. 151–168.

Archive of Our Own. "Transformative Works Organization." archiveofourown.org, 2009. Accessed 20 Feb. 2020.

Armitage, Hugh. "Whedon: 'Kitty Was the Mother of Buffy.' " Digital Spy, 1 Feb. 2019, https://www.digitalspy.com/comics/a380170/joss-whedon-kitty-pryde -was-the-mother-of-buffy/.

Beaty, Bart, and Benjamin Woo. *The Greatest Comic Book of All Time: Symbolic Capital and the Field of American Comic Books*. Palgrave, 2016.

Bechdel, Alison. *The Essential Dykes to Watch Out For*. 2008. Mariner Books, 2020.

Bechdel, Alison. *Fun Home: A Family Tragicomic*. 2006. Mariner Books, 2008.

*Black Panther*. Directed by Ryan Coogler, performances by Chadwick Boseman, Lupita Nyong'o, and Winston Duke, Marvel, 2018.

Booy, Miles. *Marvel's Mutants: The X-Men Comics of Chris Claremont*. I. B. Tauris, 2018.

Box Office Mojo. "Franchise: X-Men." www.boxofficemojo.com/franchise/fr3712454405. Accessed 12 Feb. 2021.

"Bright Lady." Marvel Database, marvel.fandom.com/wiki/Bright_Lady. Accessed 20 Feb. 2021.

Bukatman, Scott. *Matters of Gravity: Special Effects and Supermen in the 20th Century*. Duke UP, 2003.

Bumatay, Michelle. "Plural Pathways, Plural Identities." *Postcolonial Comics: Texts, Events, Identities*, edited by Binita Mehta and Pia Mukherji, Routledge, 2020, pp. 29–43.

Byrne, John, writer. *Alpha Flight*. Nos. 1–28, Marvel, 1983.

Byrne, John, writer. *Fantastic Four*. Nos. 232–295, Marvel, 1981.

Byrne, John. Response to "A Question for JB Regarding Chris Claremont." Byrne Robotics, m.byrnerobotics.com/forum/forum_posts.asp?TID=13764. Accessed 19 Feb. 2020.

Byrne, John, writer. *Sensational She-Hulk*. Nos. 1–8, Marvel, 1985.

"Callisto (comics)." Wikipedia, en.wikipedia.org/wiki/Callisto_(comics)#Being _beautiful. Accessed 4 Feb. 2021.

Campochiaro, Michael. "Blue Beetle and the Last Days of the Bronze Age." *Sequart,* 25 Aug. 2016, sequart.org/magazine/64341/blue-beetle-and-the-last-days -of-the-bronze-age/.

Campochiaro, Michael. "On X-(Wo)Men and Third-WaveFeminism." *Sequart,* 6 Feb. 2016, sequart.org/magazine/62699/on-x-women-and-third-wave-feminism/.

Campochiaro, Michael. "Word on a Wing: Claremont's Samurai Detective Colleen Wing." *Sequart,* 25 Nov. 2016, sequart.org/magazine/65181/word-on-a-wing -claremonts-samurai-detective-colleen-wing/.

Carpenter, Teresa. "Death of a Playmate." *The Village Voice,* 5 Nov. 1980.

carrington, andré m. *Speculative Blackness: The Future of Race in Science Fiction.* U of Minnesota P, 2016.

Chapman, Erin D. "Rape Fantasies and Other Assaults: Black Women's Sexuality and Racial Redemption on Film." *Black Female Sexualities,* edited by Trimiko Melancon and Joanne M. Braxton, Rutgers UP, 2015, pp. 141–158.

Chute, Hilary. *Graphic Women.* Columbia UP, 2010.

Cixous, Hélène. "The Newly Born Woman." *The Hélène Cixous Reader,* Routledge, 2003.

Claremont, Chris. Interview. *CMN,* Apr. 1978.

Claremont, Chris. Interview. Conducted by Astrid Sparks, CBR, 20 Nov. 2020, https://www.cbr.com/x-men-cyclops-chris-claremont-ruined/. Accessed 16 Feb. 2021.

Claremont, Chris. Interview. Conducted by Claire Napier, Women Write about Comics, 13 Aug. 2018, https://womenwriteaboutcomics.com/2018/08/ claremonts-consequences-discussing-asian-betsy-in-2018/. Accessed 15 Feb. 2021.

Claremont, Chris. Introduction. *The Uncanny X-Men,* vol. 5 of *Marvel Masterworks,* by Chris Claremont and John Bryne, Marvel, 2004.

Claremont, Chris. Papers, 1973–2018. Rare Manuscript Collection, Rare Book and Manuscript Library, Columbia University, New York. Accessed 20 May 2019.

Claremont, Chris, writer. *And Hellfire Is Their Name! UXM,* vol. 1, no. 132, Marvel, 1980.

Claremont, Chris, writer. *Armageddon Now. UXM,* vol. 1, no. 108, Marvel, 1977.

Claremont, Chris, writer. *The Black Dragon.* Titan Comics, 2014.

Claremont, Chris, writer. *Charge of the Light Brigade. UXM,* vol. 1, no. 218, Marvel, 1987.

Claremont, Chris, writer. *Chutes and Ladders! UXM,* vol. 1, no. 160, Marvel, 1982.

Claremont, Chris, writer. *The Cradle Will Fall. UXM,* vol. 1, no. 248, Marvel, 1989.

Claremont, Chris, writer. *Cry, Mutant! UXM,* vol. 1, no. 148, Marvel, 1981.

Claremont, Chris, writer. *Cry for the Children! UXM,* vol. 1, no. 122, Marvel, 1979.

Claremont, Chris, writer. *The Dane Curse. UXM,* vol. 1, no. 249, Marvel, 1989.

Claremont, Chris, writer. *Death by Drowning! UXM,* vol. 1, no. 221, Marvel, 1987.

Claremont, Chris, writer. *Deathstar, Rising! UXM,* vol. 1, no. 99, Marvel, 1976.

Claremont, Chris, writer. *The Doomsmith Scenario! UXM,* vol. 1, no. 94, Marvel, 1975.

Claremont, Chris, writer. *Down Under*. UXM, vol. 1, no. 229, Marvel, 1988.

Claremont, Chris, writer. *Duel*. UXM, vol. 1, no. 201, Marvel, 1985.

Claremont, Chris, writer. *Excalibur*. Nos. 1–19, Marvel, 1987.

Claremont, Chris, writer. *The Fate of the Phoenix!* UXM, vol. 1, no. 137, Marvel, 1980.

Claremont, Chris, writer. *Fever Dream*. UXM, vol. 1, no. 251, Marvel, 1989.

Claremont, Chris, writer. *Gambit: Out of the Frying Pan*. UXM, vol. 1, no. 266, Marvel, 1990.

Claremont, Chris, writer. *The Gift!* UXM, vol. 1, no. 131, Marvel, 1980.

Claremont, Chris, writer. *God Spare the Child . . .* UXM, vol. 1, no. 129, Marvel, 1979.

Claremont, Chris, writer. *Greater Love Hath No X-Man*. UXM, vol. 1, no. 100, Marvel, 1976.

Claremont, Chris, writer. *Heartbreak!* UXM, vol. 1, no. 222, Marvel, 1987.

Claremont, Chris, writer. *Home Are the Heroes!* UXM, vol. 1, no. 109, Marvel, 1977.

Claremont, Chris, writer. *Hope*. Classic X-Men, vol. 1, no. 11, Marvel, 1987.

Claremont, Chris, writer. *How Sharper Than a Serpent's Tooth . . . !* UXM, vol. 1, no. 126, Marvel, 1979.

Claremont, Chris, writer. *I Am Lady Mandarin*. UXM, vol. 1, no. 257, Marvel, 1990.

Claremont, Chris, writer. *Juggernaut's Back in Town!* UXM, vol. 1, no. 194, Marvel, 1985.

Claremont, Chris, writer. *The Key That Breaks the Locke*. UXM, vol. 1, no. 256, Marvel, 1989.

Claremont, Chris, writer. *Ladies Night*. UXM, vol. 1, no. 244, Marvel, 1989.

Claremont, Chris, writer. *Lifedeath: From the Heart of Darkness*. UXM, vol. 1, no. 198, Marvel, 1985.

Claremont, Chris, writer. *Like a Phoenix, from the Ashes*. UXM, vol. 1, no. 101, Marvel, 1976.

Claremont, Chris, writer. *Lost in the Funhouse*. UXM Annual, vol. 1, no. 11, Marvel, 1987.

Claremont, Chris, writer. *The Lower Depths*. UXM, vol. 1, no. 263, Marvel, 1990.

Claremont, Chris, writer. *Men!* Rob Liefeld, penciler. UXM, vol. 1, no. 245, Marvel, 1989.

Claremont, Chris, writer. *Merry Christmas, X-Men*. UXM, vol. 1, no. 98, Marvel, 1976.

Claremont, Chris, writer. *Mind Out of Time*. UXM, vol. 1, no. 142, Marvel, 1980.

Claremont, Chris, writer. *Night of the Demon!* UXM, vol. 1, no. 96, Marvel, 1975.

Claremont, Chris, writer. *The Path Not Taken!* UXM, vol. 1, no. 275, Marvel, 1991.

Claremont, Chris, writer. *Phoenix Unleashed!* UXM, vol. 1, no. 105, Marvel, 1977.

Claremont, Chris, writer. *Professor Xavier Is a Jerk!* UXM, vol. 1, no. 168, Marvel, 1983.

Claremont, Chris, writer. *Psylocke*. UXM, vol. 1, no. 213, Marvel, 1987.

Claremont, Chris, writer. *The Quality of Hatred*. UXM, vol. 1, no. 105, Marvel, 1979.

Claremont, Chris, writer. *Reunion*. UXM, vol. 154, no. 32, Marvel, 1981.

Claremont, Chris, writer. *Riot on Regent Street*. Captain Britain, vol. 1, no. 8, Marvel, 1976.

Claremont, Chris, writer. *Run for Your Life! UXM*, vol. 1, no. 131, Marvel, 1979.

Claremont, Chris, writer. *Something Wicked This Way Comes! UXM*, vol. 1, no. 139, Marvel, 1980.

Claremont, Chris, writer. *The Shattered Star. UXM*, vol. 1, no. 250, Marvel, 1989.

Claremont, Chris, writer. *Star 90. UXM*, vol. 1, no. 260, Marvel, 1990.

Claremont, Chris, writer. *The Submergence of Japan. UXM*, vol. 1, no. 118, Marvel, 1978.

Claremont, Chris, writer. *There's Something Awful on Muir Island! UXM*, vol. 1, no. 125, Marvel, 1979.

Claremont, Chris, writer. *To Have and Have Not. UXM*, vol. 1, no. 173. Marvel, 1983.

Claremont, Chris, writer. *To Save the Savage Land. UXM*, vol. 1, no. 116, Marvel, 1978.

Claremont, Chris, writer. *To the Ends of the Earth. New Mutants*, vol. 1, no. 32, Marvel, 1985.

Claremont, Chris, writer. *Too Late, the Heroes! UXM*, vol. 1, no. 134, Marvel, 1980.

Claremont, Chris, writer. *Uncanny X-Men*. Nos. 94–278, Marvel, 1975–1991.

Claremont, Chris, writer. *Warhunt! UXM*, vol. 1, no. 95, Marvel, 1975.

Claremont, Chris, writer. *Warhunt 2. UXM*, vol. 1, no. 193, Marvel, 1985.

Claremont, Chris, writer. *Where Duty Lies. UXM*, vol. 1, no. 219, Marvel, 1987.

Claremont, Chris, writer. *Who Will Stop the Juggernaut? UXM*, vol. 1, no. 102, Marvel, 1976.

Claremont, Chris, writer. *Why Do We Do These Things We Do? New Mutants Annual*, vol. 1, no. 2, Marvel, 1986.

Claremont, Chris, writer. *Wolverine*. Vol. 2, nos. 1–10, Marvel, 1988.

Claremont, Chris, writer. *Wolverine: Alone! UXM*, vol. 1, no. 133, Marvel, 1980.

Claremont, Chris, writer. *Wounded Wolf. UXM*, vol. 1, no. 205, Marvel, 1986.

Claremont, Chris, writer. *The "X"-Sanction. UXM*, vol. 1, no. 110, Marvel, 1978.

Claremont, Chris, writer. *X-Tinction Agenda: First Strike. UXM*, vol. 1, no. 270, Marvel, 1990.

Cocca, Carolyn. *Superwomen: Gender, Power, and Representation*. Bloomsbury Academic, 2016.

Collin, Robbie. "Bechdel Test Is Damaging to the Way We Think about Film." *Telegraph*, 15 Nov. 2013.

Connell, R. W. *Masculinities*. U of California P, 2005.

Coogan, Peter M. *Superhero: Secret Origins of a Genre*. Reynolds and Hearn, 2010.

Cooper, Carol. "Leading by Example: The Tao of Women in the X-Men World." *The Unauthorized X-Men*, edited by Len Wein, Smart Pop, 2005, pp. 183–200.

*Cosmopolitan*. "A Look Back at Burt Reynolds' Iconic Nude Photoshoot in Cosmopolitan." *Cosmopolitan*, 7 Sept. 2018, www.cosmopolitan.com /entertainment/news/a48108/burt-reynolds-cosmo-classic/.

Cresswell, J[ohn]. *Research Design*. Sage, 2014.

*Crocodile Dundee*. Directed by Peter Faiman, performances by Paul Hogan and Linda Kozlowski, Paramount Pictures, 1986.

Cronin, Brian. "Who Was the First Jewish Superhero?" CBR, 10 Feb. 2019, https://www.cbr.com/first-jewish-superhero/.

D'Agostino, Anthony Michael. " 'Flesh to Flesh Contact': Marvel Comics' Rogue and the Queer Feminist Imagination." *American Literature*, vol. 90, no. 2, 2018, pp. 251–282.

Darowski, Joseph. "When Business Improved Art." *The Ages of the X-Men: Essays on the Children of the Atom in Changing Times*, edited by J. Darowski, McFarland, 2014, pp. 37–45.

Darowski, Joseph J. *X-Men and the Mutant Metaphor: Race and Gender in the Comic Books*. Rowman and Littlefield, 2014.

Davis, Alan, writer. *It's Hard to Be a Hero*. Captain Britain, vol. 2, no. 13, Marvel, 1986.

Deane, Bradley. "Imperial Barbarians: Primitive Masculinity in Lost World Fiction." *Victorian Literature and Culture*, vol. 36, no. 1, 2008, pp. 205–225. JSTOR, www.jstor.org/stable/40347601. Accessed 24 Feb. 2021.

Dearman, N. B., and V. W. Plisko. *The Condition of Education*. National Center for Education Statistics, 1980.

DeFalco, Tom. *Comics Creators on X-Men*. Titan, 2006.

Deman, Andrew. "Busting Loose: Ms. Marvel and Post-Rape Trauma in X-Men Comics." *Journal of Graphic Novels and Comics*, vol. 11, no. 4, 2020, pp. 412–424.

Deman, Andrew. *The Margins of Comics*. Nuada, 2015.

Deman, Andrew. "A Storm of Passion: Sexual Agency and Symbolic Capital in the X-Men's Storm." *Supersex*, edited by Anna Peppard, U of Texas P, 2020, pp. 79–102.

*Dirty Harry*. Directed by Don Siegel, performances by Clint Eastwood, Andrew Robinson, and Harry Guardino, Malpaso Company, 1971.

Edidin, Jay, and Miles Stokes. *Jay and Miles X-Plain the X-Men*. https://www.xplainthexmen.com/. Accessed 25 Feb. 2021.

Eglash, Ron. "Race, Sex, and Nerds." *Social Text*, vol. 20, no. 2, Summer 2002, pp. 49–64.

*The Empire Strikes Back*. Directed by Irvine Kershner, performances by Mark Hamill, Harrison Ford, and Carrie Fisher, 20th Century Fox, 1980.

Englehart, Steve, writer. *Avengers*, vol. 1, nos. 105–152. Marvel, 1972–1976.

Eriksen, Neil. "Pop Culture and Revolutionary Theory: Understanding Punk Rock." *Theoretical Review*, no. 18, Sept.–Oct. 1980, n.p.

Fawaz, Ramzi. *The New Mutants: Superheroes and the Radical Imagination of American Comics*. NYU P, 2016.

Franklin, G. "Olivier Assayas on Cinema and Superhero Films." Dark Horizons, 30 Dec. 2019, https://www.darkhorizons.com/olivier-assayas-on-cinema-superhero-films/. Accessed 27 Dec. 2021.

Friedan, Betty. *The Feminine Mystique*. 1963. W. W. Norton, 2013.

Friedman, Marilyn. "Autonomy and Social Relationships: Rethinking the Feminist Critique." *Feminists Rethink the Self*, edited by Diana Tietjens Meyers, Westview Press, 1997, pp. 40–61.

Gaiman, Neil (@neilhimself). "It is great to see Chris Claremont getting his dues. Modern tv owes so much to him." Twitter, 22 Feb. 2019, 8:09 a.m.

Galvan, Margaret. "From Kitty to Cat: Kitty Pryde and the Phases of Feminism." *The Ages of the X-Men: Essays on the Children of the Atom in Changing Times*, edited by Joseph J. Darowski, McFarland, 2014, pp. 46–62.

Gillis, Peter. *Strikeforce: Morituri*. No. 13, Marvel, 1987.

Glenday, Craig. *Guinness World Records 2011*. Bantam Books, 2011.

*The Godfather*. Directed by Francis Ford Coppola, performances by Al Pacino, James Caan, and Marlon Brando, Paramount, 1972.

Grzanka, Patrick R. Introduction. *Intersectionality: A Foundations and Frontiers Reader*, edited by Patrick R. Grzanka, Routledge, 2014, pp. 1–24.

Haggard, H. Rider, and David Maule. *King Solomon's Mines*. Pearson Education, 2000.

Hanks, Fletcher, and Paul Karasik. *You Shall Die by Your Own Evil Creation!* Fantagraphics Books, 2010.

Harraway, Donna. "A Cyborg Manifesto." *Simians, Cyborgs, and Women: The Reinvention of Nature*, edited by D. Harraway, Routledge, 1991, pp. 149–181.

Harris-Perry, Melissa. Foreword. *Black Female Sexualities*, edited by Trimiko Melancon and Joanne M. Braxton, Rutgers UP, 2015, pp. viii–xi.

Hatfield, Charles. *Alternative Comics: An Emerging Literature*. UP of Mississippi, 2006.

Helvie, Forrest. "The Bechdel Test and a Sexy Lamp: Detecting Gender Bias and Stereotypes in Mainstream Comics." Sequart, sequart.org/magazine/34150 /the-bechdel-test-and-a-sexy-lamp-detecting-gender-bias-and-stereotypes-in -mainstream-comics/. Accessed 15 Feb. 2021.

Hogan, Patrick C. *Sexual Identities: A Cognitive Literary Study*. Oxford UP, 2018.

Homer. *The Iliad*. Franklin Library, 1976.

hooks, bell. *Ain't I a Woman: Black Women and Feminism*. Routledge, 2015.

hooks, bell. *The Will to Change: Men, Masculinity, and Love*. Washington Square Press, 2005.

Howe, Sean. *Marvel Comics: The Untold Story*. Harper, 2013.

Irigaray, Luce. *This Sex Which Is Not One*. Cornell UP, 1985.

Johnson, Brian. "Dazzler, Melodrama, and Shame: Mutant Allegory, Closeted Readers." *Supersex*, edited by Anna Peppard, U of Texas P, 2020, pp. 103–128.

Kendall, Lori. "Nerd Nation: Images of Nerds in U.S. Popular Culture." *International Journal of Cultural Studies*, vol. 2, no. 2, Aug. 1999, pp. 260–283.

Kerns, Susan. "I'd Like Everything That's Bad for Me: Tank Girl's Cracks in Patriarchal Pop Culture." *The Routledge Companion to Gender and Sexuality in Comic Book Studies*, edited by Frederick L. Aldama, Routledge, 2021, pp. 341–351.

Kirtley, Susan. "A Word to You Feminist Women: The Parallel Legacies of Feminism and Underground Comics." *The Cambridge History of the Graphic Novel*, edited by Jan Baetens et al., Cambridge UP, 2018, pp. 269–285.

Lam, Anna. "Taking a Dip in the Crazy Pool: The Evolution of X-Women from Heroic Subject to Sexual Object." *The Journal of Research on Libraries and Young Adults*, 22 Apr. 2013, www.yalsa.ala.org/jrlya/2013/04/taking-a-dip-in-the -crazy-pool-the-evolution-of-x-women-from-heroic-subject-to-sexual-object/. Accessed 16 Feb. 2021.

Langsdale, Samantha. "The Dark Phoenix as 'Promising Monster.'" *Comics and Sacred Texts*, edited by Assaf Gamzou and Ken Koltun-Fromm, UP of Mississippi, 2018, pp. 153–171.

Layton, Bob, and Jackson Guice. *Third Genesis*. X-Factor, vol. 1, no. 1, Marvel, 1986.

Lee, Stan, writer. *The Return of the Blob!* X-Men, vol. 1, no. 7, Marvel, 1964.

Lee, Stan, writer. *X-Men*, vol. 1, nos. 1–11, Marvel, 1963–1965.

*Legion*. Created by Noah Hawley, performances by Dan Stevens, Jean Smart, and Rachel Keller, FX, 2017–2019.

Le Guin, Ursula K. "American SF and the Other." *Language of the Night: Essays on Fantasy and Science Fiction*, edited by Susan Wood, HarperCollins, 1992, 97–100.

Lorde, Audre. "Age, Race, Class, and Sex: Women Redefining Difference." *Literary Theory: An Anthology*, edited by Julie Rivkin and Michael Ryan, Blackwell, 2004, pp. 630–636.

Lovatt, Helen. "The Eloquence of Dido: Exploring Speech and Gender in Virgil's *Aeneid*." *Dictynna*, vol. 10, no. 29, Nov. 2013, http://journals.openedition.org /dictynna/993. Accessed 19 Feb. 2020.

Mahn, Gerri. "Fatal Attractions: Wolverine, the Hegemonic Male and the Crisis of Masculinity in the 1990s." *The Ages of the X-Men: Essays on the Children of the Atom in Changing Times*, edited by Joseph J. Darowski, McFarland, 2014, pp. 116–127.

Mantlo, Bill, writer. "A Friend in Need." *Alpha Flight*, vol. 1, no. 33, Marvel, 1985.

Mantlo, Bill, writer. "Honor." *Alpha Flight*, vol. 1, no. 34, Marvel, 1986.

*Marvel's Behind the Mask*. Directed by Mike Jacobs, Disney+, Feb. 2021.

Marx, Christy. "Why I Didn't Grow Up to Be Marvel Girl." *The Unauthorized X-Men*, edited by Len Wein and Leah Wilson, Ben Bella Books, 2006, pp. 171–182.

Meaney, Patrick. Interview by Julius Darius. Sequart, sequart.org/magazine /21187/patrick-meaney-the-sequart-interview/.

Milgrom, Al. *Editori-Al. Marvel Fanfare*, no. 2, Marvel, 1982.

Miller, Frank, writer. *Daredevil*. Vol. 1, nos. 168–191, Marvel, 1980–1983.

Miller, Frank, writer. *Daredevil*. Vol. 1, nos. 226–233, Marvel, 1986.

Miller, Nicholas E. "'Is There Anything Left to Be Shattered?' Reading Dazzler in the #MeToo Moment." *The Middle Spaces*, 22 July 2020, themiddlespaces .com/2018/04/10/dazzler-in-the-metoo-moment/. Accessed 23 Feb. 2021.

Moench, Doug, writer. *Master of Kung Fu*. Vol. 1, nos. 20–120, Marvel, 1974.

Moench, Doug, writer. *Moon Knight*. Vol. 1, nos. 1–33, Marvel, 1980.

Mulvey, Laura. "Visual Pleasure and Narrative Cinema." *Visual and Other Pleasures*, by L. Mulvey, Palgrave MacMillan, 1989, pp. 14–28.

*The New Mutants*. Directed by Josh Boone, performances by Anya Taylor-Joy, Charlie Heaton, and Blu Hunt, 20th Century Fox, 2020.

Nietzsche, Friedrich W. *The Birth of Tragedy: And, the Genealogy of Morals*. 1872. Anchor Books, 1990.

Oyola, Osvaldo. "Imperfect Storm (Part Two): Exploring 'Lifedeath II.'" *The Middle Spaces*, 14 July 2020, themiddlespaces.com/2015/07/14/imperfect-storm-part-two/.

Palmer, Lorrie. "The Punisher as Revisionist Superhero Western." *The Superhero Reader*, edited by Charles Hatfield et al., UP of Mississippi, 2013, pp. 279–294.

Peppard, Anna. "Blue Becomings: Revisiting Excalibur no. 4." *The Middle Spaces*, 15 June 2021 https://themiddlespaces.com/2021/05/11/excalibur-4/.

Peppard, Anna. "Chris Claremont laid the groundwork . . ." @ClaremontRun, 10 Mar. 2022.

Peppard, Anna. Introduction. *Supersex*, edited by A. Peppard, U of Texas P, 2020, pp. 103–128.

Peppard, Anna. "The Power of the Marvel(ous) Image: Reading Excess in the Styles of Todd McFarlane, Jim Lee, and Rob Liefeld." *Journal of Graphic Novels and Comics*, vol. 10, no. 3, 2019, pp. 320–341.

Powell, Jason. *The Best There Is at What He Does: Examining Chris Claremont's X-Men*. Sequart, 2016.

Reynolds, Richard. *Super Heroes: A Modern Mythology*. UP of Mississippi, 1994.

Riviere, Joan. "Womanliness as a Masquerade." *International Journal of Psychoanalysis*, vol. 10, 1929, pp. 303–313.

Rivkin, Julie, and Michael Ryan. "Feminist Paradigms." *Literary Theory: An Anthology*, edited by J. Rivkin and M. Ryan, Blackwell, 2004, pp. 515–526.

Robinson, Lillian S. *Wonder Women: Feminism Zaps the Comics*. Routledge, 2004.

Sabin, Roger. *Comics, Comix and Graphic Novels*. Phaidon, 2014.

Schad-Seifert, Annette. "Samurai and Sarariiman: The Discourse on Masculinity in Modern Japan." *Can Japan Globalize?*, edited by Arne Holzhausen, Physica Heidelberg, 2001, pp. 199–211.

Schedeen, Jesse. "Marvel Comics and History." IGN, 7 Mar. 2011, ca.ign.com/articles/2011/03/07/marvel-comics-and-history. Accessed 22 Feb. 2021.

Shooter, James, Frank Springer, and Vince Colletta. *Dazzler: The Movie*. Marvel Comics Group, 1984.

Shooter, Jim, Ann Nocenti, and Kim DeMulder. *X-Men: Beauty and the Beast*. Marvel, 2012.

Shyminsky, Neil. "Mutant Readers Reading Mutants: Appropriation, Assimilation, and the X-Men." *International Journal of Comic Art*, vol. 8, 2006, pp. 387–405.

Shyminsky, Neil. "Mutation, Racialization, Decimation." *Unstable Masks: Whiteness and American Superhero Comics*, edited by Sean Guynes and Martin Lund, Ohio State UP, 2020, pp. 158–173.

Simone, Gail. "Women in Refrigerators." 1999. Lby3.com, http://www.lby3.com/wir/. Accessed 15 Feb. 2019.

Simone, Gail (@GailSimone). "Important to note that the biggest sea change in female superheroes ever came from Marvel, with the X-men. I think that changed the rules for the better for everyone." Twitter, 6 Oct. 2020, 3:49 a.m.

Smith, Colin. "On Alan Moore's Wildc.a.t.s." Sequart, 20 Mar. 2012, sequart.org/magazine/10679/on-alan-moore-wildcats/.

Sobel, Eric. "The Whitest There Is at What I Do: Japanese Identity and the Unmarked Hero in *Wolverine* (1982)." *Unstable Masks: Whiteness and American Superhero Comics*, edited by Sean Guynes et al., Ohio State UP, 2020, pp. 226–241.

Sontag, Susan. *On Photography*. Allen Lane, 1978.

Spillers, Hortense J. "Mama's Baby, Papa's Maybe: An American Grammar Book." *Culture and Countermemory: The "American" Connection*, a special issue of *Diacritics*, vol. 17, no. 2, Summer 1987, pp. 64–81.

Starr, Charlie W. "The Best There Is . . . Isn't Very Nice." *The Unauthorized X-Men*, edited by Len Wein, Smart Pop, 2005, pp. 65–78.

Steinem, Gloria. Introduction. *Wonder Woman*, edited by William Moulton Marston, Holt, Reinhart, and Winston, 1972, pp. 1–4.

Tennyson, Alfred. *The Idylls of the King*. Velhagen and Klasing, 1926.

Tylor, E. B. *Primitive Culture*. 1871. Harper, 1974.

Virgil. *Aeneid*. Yale UP, 2021.

Wanzo, Rebecca. "It's a Hero? Black Comics and Satirizing Subjection." *The Blacker the Ink: Constructions of Black Identity in Comics and Sequential Art*, edited by Frances Gateward and John Jennings, Rutgers UP, 2015, pp. 317–332.

Warwick, Lynda. "Feminist Wicca." *Women and Therapy*, vol. 16, pp. 2–3, 121–133, doi:10.1300/J015v16n02_13. Accessed 25 Feb. 2021.

Wein, Len, writer. *Deadly Genesis! Giant-Size X-Men*, vol. 1, no. 1, Marvel, 1975.

Wein, Len, writer. *Giant-Size X-Men*. Vol. 1, no. 1, Marvel, 1975.

Wein, Len, writer. *Incredible Hulk*. Vol. 1, nos. 180–181, Marvel, 1974.

Wells, H. G. *The Time Machine*. Signet, 2014.

Whaley, Deborah E. *Black Women in Sequence: Re-inking Comics, Graphic Novels, and Anime*. U of Washington P, 2016.

White, Mark D. "Is Suicide Always Immoral? Jean Grey, Immanuel Kant, and the Dark Phoenix Saga." *X-Men and Philosophy*, edited by William Irwin et al., John Wiley and Sons, 2009, pp. 27–37.

Windsor-Smith, Barry. *Marvel Comics Presents*. Vol. 1, nos. 72–84, Marvel, 1991.

*X-Men: Dark Phoenix*. Directed by Simon Kinberg, performances by Michael Fassbender, Sophie Turner, and James McAvoy, 20th Century Fox, 2019.

*X-Men: The Animated Series*. Created by Larry Houston et al., performances by Cedric Smith, Cal Dodd, and Lenore Zann, 20th Century Fox, 1992.

Zenari, Vivian. "Mutant Mutandis: The X-Men's Wolverine and the Construction of Canada." *Nationalisms*, edited by James Gifford and Gabrielle Zezulka-Mailloux, CRC Humanities Studio, 2003, pp. 53–67.

# Index

Page numbers marked with an *f* indicate figures in text. Comic book characters do not have their names inverted but are alphabetized under first names.

commercial value influencing depiction of, 86–87; emotional hysterics of, 79, 80; emotional vulnerability of with Jean Grey, 81–83, 94; gender subversiveness of, 77, 81, 86; hegemonic (white) masculinity and, 74–77; as leader of the X-Men, 43–44, 76–78, 81, 82; masculine stereotype undermined by, 77, 87; noncombative physical contact by, 14–15, 15*f*; optic blasts and erotic energies of, 30, 84; out-of-costume to in-costume ratio of, 65*f*; patriarchal culture explored by, 22, 74–77, 84–85, 86–87; personifying crisis of masculinity for, 22, 84; physical representation of, 16*f*; in *Proteus Saga*, 25; relationship of with Jean Grey, 22, 28–29, 30–31, 73–74, 77–79, 80–85; relationship of with Storm, 43, 44; sense of duty of vs. internal desires, 79, 80, 87; sexual competition of with Mastermind over Jean Grey, 85–86; symbolic emasculation of, 30, 84–86; as viewpoint character, 16, 44

Sean Cassidy/Banshee, 15*f*, 24, 25*f*, 37*f*, 99–100

sex roles. *See* gender roles explored, overview

sexuality: agency and, 31, 83–85, 85*f*, 45–46, 48–49, 29–30; black female, 36, 37–38; bodily trauma and, 30; *Dark Phoenix Saga*, 31; female gaze and, 123–124; female desire and, 31, 46; and fetishization of women in comics, 17–18; male gaze and, 17–18, 123; monstrosity and, 31, 32; platonic relationships and, 122–123; Psylocke as sex symbol, 55; repression and, 31–32; sex appeal and victimhood, 66–70; and sexual commodification of men, 123–124; and sexual spectacle, 123; and sexual sublimation in *X-Men*, 30; sexual subtext, 30; sexual violence, 36; superpowers and, 94. *See also* femininity; masculinity, hegemonic; nudity; *individual characters*

Shadowcat/Kitty Pryde. *See* Kitty Pryde/ Shadowcat

Shooter, Jim, 27, 64, 66, 67, 81, 87
Shyminsky, Neil, 75, 94–95
Silvestri, Mark, 70
Simone, Gail, 1–2
Smith, Colin, 138
Smith, Paul, 123
Sobel, Eric, 104, 105
Sontag, Susan, 134
Sparks, Astrid, 87
Spillers, Hortense, 13
Starr, Charlie, 90, 93
Steinem, Gloria, 18–19
Stokes, Miles, 3
Storm. *See* Ororo Munroe/Storm
*Stranger Things*, 139
Stratten, Dorothy, 66
*Super Heroes: A Modern Mythology* (Reynolds), 39
superpowers, 94–96, 96*f*, 117

Thunderbird/John Proudstar. *See* John Proudstar/Thunderbird
Tylor, E. B., 103

*Uncanny X-Men* issues and storylines: *Acts of Vengeance* storyline, 55, 62–63; *Dark Phoenix Saga* storyline, 27–29, 31–33, 46, 83–84; *Days of Future Past* storyline, 42–43; *God Loves, Man Kills* (Marvel Graphic Novel no. 5) storyline, 122; *Inferno* storyline, 130; *Mutant Massacre* storyline, 47; ; *Proteus Saga* storyline, 25–26

—numbered storylines: no. 1 *X-Men*, 76, 97; no. 21 *Duel*, 125; no. 94 *The Doomsmith Scenario*, 77; no. 95 *Warhunt!*, 77; no. 96 *Night of the Demon*, 77–78; no. 98 *Merry Christmas, X-Men*, 78, 119; no. 99 *Deathstar, Rising!*, 119; no. 100 *Greater Love Hath No X-Man*, 79, 80; no. 101 *Like a Phoenix, from the Ashes*, 80–81; no. 102 *Who Will Stop the Juggernaut*, 81; no. 105 *Phoenix Unleashed!*, 81; no. 106 *The "X"-Sanction*, 82; no. 109 *Home are the Heroes!*, 81–82, 99; no. 116 *To Save the Savage Land*, 99–100; no. 118 *The Submergence of Japan*, 98; no. 122 *Cry for*